IT GIVES ME GREAT PLEASURE: PUBLIC SPEAKING MADE FUN & EASY

by

Gary Michael
The Talk Doc

It Gives Me Great Pleasure
copyright © 1996 by Gary Michael

published by
Talk Doc Books
3009 E. 10th Avenue
Denver, CO 80206
(303) 321-6607

Cover design by Jerry Spaeder
Cover drawing by Gary Michael

To my students and clients who
honored me with their presence
and taught me by their example.

Thanks to

Gordon Pierce for encouragement and counsel,
Fred Holden for the kick in the pants that jarred
me from my role of writer to that of publisher,
Hank Kugeler for his surgical editorial eye,
Perry Fisher and Max Dixon for valuable
suggestions, and
DeAnne Minner for long hours of layout labor.

TABLE OF CONTENTS

Prologue   ix

Why Make Presentations Anyway?   1

The Four Types of Talks   4

Things To Know about Your Audience   6
    Respect for Listeners
    Eleven Things It Helps To Know

How To Prepare Your Introducer   14

Putting a Speech Together   18
    • Structure Is Important
    • Provide Cues for Your Audience
    • Never Read Your Speech
    • How To Compose Your Speech
    • Reinforce Important Points

Ways To Begin   27
    • Start Out Lively
    • Be Real
    • Save Your Thanks until the End
    • How To Organize a Story
    • Start with a Startling Statistic
    • Open with a Quote
    • Pose a Question

Delivery   36
    Be Authentic
    Seven Tips for Conveying Sincerity

Your Voice   46

Pause Power   48

Handling Nervousness   51
    • Nervousness Is Natural
    • Preparation
    • Breathing
    • Exercise

Making Important Points:
Ways To Gain Emphasis   55

Your Body   57
    • Body Language Speaks Louder than Words
    • Relax Yourself To Relax Your Listeners
    • Movement Adds Interest
    • Exxagerate Your Movements for Larger
      Audiences
    • Gestures Can Aid or Distract
    • Focus on What You're Saying
    • Fluidity

Persuasion   67
    • The Most Difficult Speech To Give
    • Changing a Person's Beliefs or Actions
    • Appeal to Reason
    • Tell a Story
    • The Emotional Element

Audience Relations   78
    • Connect with the Audience
    • Share the Stage

Audio/Visual Advice   85
    • TV Has Changed Us
    • Audio/Visuals Aid Presentations

Handouts   89
    • To Give or Not To Give Handouts
    • Points To Consider about Handouts

Games That Enliven Presentations   92

Impromptu   105
    • Impromptu Speeches Can Be as
      Fun as Games
    • Imaginative Impromptu Speeches
    • Serious Impromptu Speeches
    • IPAC Formula

Quotes Of Note: 109
Wise Words To Use as Openers, Closers and In-
Betweeners

On Becoming Who We Truly Are:
Authenticity as Presence and Responsibility 116

The Talk Doc's Twelve Tips for
Powerful, Passionate Presentations   119

PROLOGUE

Winston Churchill was one of the most powerful speakers of this century. Yet he claimed never to say "It gives me great pleasure..." when addressing an audience. Only a few things gave him intense pleasure, he said, and speaking was not among them.

On at least one occasion, however, Mr. Churchill violated his stated policy. He organized an informal group called the Other Club for the discussion of ideas and politics. An impromptu speech was a standard practice of the club. The members names went into one hat, topics into another. A name and topic were drawn, and that person spoke on that topic. Once Churchill's name was drawn with the topic "Sex." Churchill rose, pointed to the card and said, "It gives me great pleasure," and sat back down.

Unlike Churchill, I have long found public speaking an extraordinary pleasure. Composing and delivering a presentation (whether called a speech, talk, lecture or address) is a thrilling experience. It has both a literary and a performance dimension. Both require creativity. Here's an opportunity for self-expression that benefits others. Through the ideas they share and the way they share them, speakers can touch people at deep levels and cause them to think in new ways. Good speakers literally change people's lives.

A speaker is like a singer/songwriter or playwright/actor in that he or she both brings about and communicates something important, something that can expand an audience's vision, understanding and range of experience. A speaker can bring something new to the world, can actively participate in that on-goingness which is the life of thought and of civilization.

That's why speaking gives me great pleasure—and because it's fun. My first contact with that fun was as a child. My mother taught me a little recitation about a boy named Ben Oak, who always said "huh" when anyone spoke. At age four, I recited it in front of military troops stationed at a Denver base. Their delight in my performance—and the praise that came with it—made me happy. I understood early on that by entertaining people one can earn their admiration. Thus began a life-long love affair with the spoken word.

Chapter 1
WHY MAKE PRESENTATIONS ANYWAY?

In an often-referenced survey, many people claimed that speaking in public was their greatest fear, even greater than their fear of death. Old as the research is, it's still safe to assume that a lot of people become paralyzed at the prospect of speaking in public. In the college-level Speech Communication classes I taught, I was surprised at how terrified people were to stand up and deliver even a brief anecdotal introduction of themselves. These were adult students, mind you, people in their thirties and forties who held responsible jobs in the corporate world. Some couldn't say their name without shaking.

We all make presentations every day. When we exchange words with a friend, request something of a waiter, or coax a child to go to school, we're presenting ideas, aiming for action, or hoping for a laugh. Why, then, the fear of public speaking? What is so different about a bigger audience of people we haven't met yet?

The difference, I think, has more to do with the fact that the people are unknown to us than how many of them there are. Most folks would feel more comfortable standing before forty people at a family reunion and eulogizing Greatgranpa than asking fifteen strangers in a boardroom to sponsor a volunteer program. The reunion is a supportive crowd. A eulogy carries no risk of rejection. In the boardroom we're subject to judgment. The audience doesn't start out on our side. Our own and others' future interests may be at stake. Just thinking about it makes us nervous.

Therein lies not only a reason for doing public speaking, but a clue as to how we can combat the fear. Courage is not the absence of fear. To have no fear one would have to be either crazy or very stupid. Courage is the willingness to take action in the face of fear, refusing to succumb to it. This doesn't mean that fear is overcome in the sense that it disappears. It means that we shoulder our fear and march forward. We act fearless. One result of acting, fear it as we may, is that we feel better about ourselves when we do it well. To be afraid and act in spite of that fear can be an exhilarating experience, one that lends us courage to do the same thing the next time a fear of something threatens to intimidate us.

As a kid I was afraid to pole vault. Other boys in my class launched their bodies into the air and landed safely in the sand, whether or not they cleared the bar. I was so terrified that I'd fall back onto the unpadded approach that I simply never tried to pole vault. For that matter, I wouldn't even play catcher in a baseball game for fear that a foul tip would evade my mitt and hit me.

As a result of these fears I never faced down, I grew up with a chicken complex. Despite achievements as a high school and college athlete in tennis and track, a ghost lurked in my soul. Something was missing from my manhood. So in my mid-twenties, I took up rock climbing and made myself do climbs that literally had me shaking in my shoes. Only then did I forgive myself for being the chicken I was as a kid. Even after a fall fractured my skull in two places, it didn't occur to me that I might be over-compensating. By then, rock climbing had become too much fun. This brings me to another reason to speak in public: **Fun.**

Speaking to people is one of the most exciting things I've ever done. In a way it's even more exciting than climbing rocks, riding rapids or jumping from an airplane. What makes it so is that it benefits other people. We do daredevil recreations for our own benefit—to prove ourselves, experience thrills, feed our self-esteem. No one else is better off for our having scaled a vertical wall or skied a double-black run. As speakers, we have the opportunity to share ourselves, to enrich someone else's life, to make a gift to people of what we know. They may be able to incorporate it into their own lives and then in turn pass it on to others.

The Socratic dictum, "The unexamined life is not worth living," may be a bit overstated. Yet there's no doubt that by sharing ourselves as speakers, we learn more about ourselves. Organizing and analyzing ideas forces us to question them in ways we otherwise would not. Our thinking becomes more focused, sharpened, critical. New insights and avenues occur to us. We attempt to relate personal experiences to abstract concepts, giving more meaning to the concepts, validating them. When we can't think of examples that demonstrate the validity of an idea, or we find some that fly in the face of it, we reject them. This process is one of self-discovery, of finding out not only what we believe, but more importantly, why.

Chapter 2
FOUR TYPES OF TALKS

Every public address falls into one of four basic categories.

Informative talks aim at edification. The most common example is a typical lecture to a class by a college professor.

Entertaining talks are usually humorous and have no goal beyond amusement. A good example is stand-up comedy.

Persuasive talks have as their goal some action to be taken by the listener, even if the action is simply a change of attitude. We are bombarded by persuasive talks every day, especially if we watch television or listen to radio. Commercials, no matter how subtle or understated, are attempts to get us do something—buy a particular product or vote for a candidate or amendment.

Motivational speaking is a kind of persuasion. A motivational or inspirational speaker persuades people to feel a particular way, usually better about themselves and their potential. The same strategies that apply to persuasive speaking apply to motivational speaking. The most significant difference is that a motivational speech need not call for a specific action or belief on the part of the audience. A more positive attitude or greater enthusiasm suffices.

These four basic types are rarely found in a pure and absolute form. More often, a speech is a hybrid consisting of two or more of the four basic types.

An informative talk often contains humor, and it may so inspire a listener that he or she decides to join the military, become a marine biologist or stop having children. But the primary intent of the talk is simply to disseminate data, explicate ideas, or leave the audience better informed than when the talk began.

An entertaining talk may contain information, misinformation (more charitably called exaggeration), real-life or made-up stories. Any one of these may prompt some action by a listener, even if it's only to repeat a joke. But the speaker's intent is to entertain the audience. Other results are purely ancillary.

Persuasive talks contain at least some information, as we discuss in Chapter 13. Good persuasive talks are also entertaining. That's what keeps the average audience interested.

Although I enjoy a well-delivered motivational talk, I am suspicious of their long-term results. The best of them are little more than artful pep talks, often entertaining but not likely to change people's lives in significant and lasting ways. I prefer to hear solid information and practical steps I can take to achieve a goal—simple how-to stuff. For me, real motivation comes from within. To all who benefit from jump starts and all who make a living giving them, my apologies.

Chapter 3
THINGS TO KNOW ABOUT YOUR AUDIENCE

Respect Your Listeners
Every audience is sacred. That's the most important thing to know about any audience. Take the axiom seriously and you'll welcome the opportunity to do some homework and put forth the extra effort to prepare your speech and customize it for each individual audience.

Ten Things It Helps To Know
Important audience characteristics to consider in your preparation are:

1. Age
    Current coinages or slang that may endear you to a young audience could be lost on an older one. Retired people talk mostly to other retired people and aren't likely to know that "wicked" can be a term of praise. Young people aren't as likely to know medical terms for maladies that afflict the elderly as are older people. They may think "colostomy" is a form of government.
    The older a crowd, the more conservative it's likely to be. That means we exercise more discretion in our choice of language. Eliminate phrases that derive from body parts or functions from presentations to older audiences. Some examples are: "pissed off," "lacking balls," "shorts in a bunch," and "shot the wad."

Older people often have hearing problems and require more volume from the speaker or sound system. They may also require more frequent rest and relief breaks.

2. Knowledge of the Subject

Are you talking to experts or novices? When I speak at a Toastmasters meeting, I address one aspect of public speaking in as much depth as time allows. When I teach a three-hour crash course to people who are terrified to speak in public, I give only a few basic ideas and a chance to practice them.

3. Religion

Unless a religious group requests your services, you probably have a variety of religious beliefs in the average audience. The wisest policy is to speak no ill of any religion. If you must touch on a religious issue, do so delicately.

4. Race and Ethnicity

Even before it became popular to debunk political correctness, I loved ethnic humor. Stereotypes are only dangerous if we take them seriously. One way not to take them seriously is to utilize them in humor. While I love a good ethnic, racial or so-called sexist story, I never tell one to anyone but trusted friends. Even telling one as an example of something *not to do* can get a speaker in trouble.

We live in a time when a lot of people are looking for ways to be victims. Anything that even indirectly suggests stereotyping raises a red flag. The same joke that gets laughter when a minority member tells it to other members of the minority can bring condemnation when it is issued from the lips of someone who is not part of the minority. Sure, that's hypocritical, but it's one of those hypocrisies we do well to live around.

5. Occupation

A group of engineers will respond better to detail than will abstract expressionist painters. A subtle distinction is more readily grasped by members of a profession who deal with such things, such as lawyers, than by nuts and bolts professions, such as plumbers. Sports analogies and metaphors that make a hit at a coaches convention will be less effective at a meeting of metaphysicians. A literary allusion that elicits nods and chuckles from English professors may bring blank stares from dental hygienists.

6. Education

The rules for education are related to, yet not the same as, the rules for occupation. I'm always surprised when someone compliments me on my vocabulary. It doesn't strike me as anything special. What seems like ordinary language to a Ph.D. may well overwhelm someone who didn't go to college.

One school of thought advocates "dumb guy proofing" your every presentation: take out any word that may confuse or bewilder even one member of the audience. While that person wonders what the word meant, you have moved on and lost him. If the person asks someone seated beside him what the word means, the interruption may cause the second person to miss some of your message.

I respect the rationale for dumb guy proofing but do not practice it. One of the things people get when they hire me is my background, education and vocabulary. If I dumb guy proof my speech, I cheat the audience of an important part of me and my message. Were it not for speakers who used words I was unfamiliar with, I would not have the vocabulary I do today. Those speakers became occasions for my learning new ideas and new words. They did me a favor. If I can do a similar favor for others, it's my duty to do so.

7. Socioeconomic Status

"What's the difference if people are wealthy or poor?" you may ask. "We're all just people, especially in a democratic nation." That's a fine sentiment, very egalitarian. However, if you know the financial resources of your audience, it can be a cue to the suitability of examples and anecdotes. For example, we put needless distance between ourselves and our audience if we talk about a trip, possession, or membership in a club few of them could afford.

I vividly remember a scene in the movie *Terms of Endearment*. Shirley MacLaine instructs two workmen to take care when hanging a small painting by Auguste Renoir in her daughter's hospital room. "It's worth more than either of you will make in your lifetime," she says. The workmen looked pained over this needless expression of her superior wealth.

By the same token, if a speaker were to dwell on his or her impoverished childhood, it could turn off an audience of affluent people who came by their affluence via family fortunes rather than hard work. People who become wealthy either by birth or by marrying into a wealthy family do not understand the difficulties of earning a living in the way working people do. Similarly, so-called self-made individuals, especially those who did not go to college, will not respond enthusiastically to a talk on the importance of a college education. A friend of mine who made the mistake of giving such a talk to that kind of audience said she was so devastated by the reception it got that she sat in her car afterward and cried for half an hour.

Knowing the socioeconomic status of an audience also gives you an idea of how to dress. If you wear a $2,000 suit to talk to members of the Teamsters Union, it could make you appear elitist or, worse, like someone who has never gotten grease on his hands. The same suit will command respect from a group of well-to-do entrepreneurs or successful investors.

While we're on the subject of dress, I have an unorthodoxy to utter. I think dress is the most overrated element of making a good impression. To be sure, people judge you by your apparel before you've had a chance to open your mouth. The judgment they make on the basis of your appearance, unless you're in ragged or smelly clothes, is quickly overwhelmed by the impression you make as a speaker and person. Who would you rather listen to, a finely dressed, perfectly groomed jerk who is poorly informed and a weak speaker or an unfashionably outfitted, unkempt individual who delivers a dynamite, thought-provoking address?

If you're not as willing as I to flaunt convention, here's the conventional wisdom.

Dressing well, which means suitably for the occasion, gives you a leg up on credibility. Dressed "suitably for the occasion" means wearing clothes similar to those worn by the audience, except, of course, specialty uniforms such as military and monastic attire. If you don't know how your audience will be dressed, ask. If you have to guess, risk erring on the side of dressiness. It is better to be a little overdressed than under. People are likely to be flattered that you dressed up for them and are quicker to forgive foppishness than excess informality. The overdressed person has the advantage of appearing to want to look his best and doesn't run the risk of letting the audience think that he doesn't take them seriously.

Once you have credibility, you can wear what you like, and people will listen. Tony Robbins could wear a gunny sack and listeners would rush to touch its hem. Until you have Tony's skill and following, I don't recommend a gunny sack. Clean, comfortable clothes that don't call too much attention to themselves will do.

If you prefer bright color because it feels like "you," wear it. Just remember, many people are suspicious of unfamiliar outfits. I once wore a pair of leather pants, the dressiest pants in my wardrobe, to speak at a business lunch. To me, they connoted class and respect for the audience. A year after the fact, someone who had been in the audience confided to me that those pants left many audience members wondering if I knew to whom I was speaking. They thought that I had mistaken a group of business owners for a ranchers association.

When you start to talk, the focus quickly shifts from your clothes to your vocal and intellectual appearance, your sincerity, knowledge and presentation style. These are more integral to who

11

you are than what you wear. People will soon forget your clothes and long remember what kind of speaker you are. "Power suits are only as powerful as the people inside them." A corporate executive said that. "Look to thy soul before thy suit." I said that. Of course, as Dennis Miller likes to say, it's just my opinion. I could be wrong.

8. Lifestyles

People who have had an experience similar to one you describe are likely to relate more strongly to your story. Golf stories entertain golfers more than rock climbers. While many of us respond well to most any good adventure story, it's better to tell such a story in a way that suggests anyone in the audience could, with sufficient determination, undertake such an adventure. An adventure that requires inordinate wealth, physical strength, or specialized skill will be less interesting than one ordinary folks can actually envision themselves participating in—if only imaginatively.

9. Expectations

Give every audience what it would like to get from you, not what you would like to give them. Ask in advance what they'd like to get from your presentation—new information, a few laughs, advice, or the opportunity to question you. Get to the presentation early and talk to audience members. Doing your audience this favor is one of the biggest favors you can do for yourself.

Some speakers send a list of questions to audience members in advance of the program. If you do this, include a SASE or you'll have wasted time, paper and postage. I prefer to phone a few of the people who will be present and elicit input. It's more personal, gets me better information, and becomes an occasion for advance bonding.

If you know what the audience doesn't want or expect, it can be as important as knowing what they do expect. Not long ago, I was present at a professional association meeting where a nationally known speaker gave the keynote address. Instead of the informative talk the audience looked forward to, the speaker did what amounted to an infomercial. He had a self-help course to hawk and hawk he did. In another forum, his action might have been perfectly acceptable to the audience. In this situation, trying to sell a course—or anything else—to a group that came wanting only to learn was a serious mistake. It cost the speaker a lot of goodwill.

If you want to sell something—tapes, books, donuts or advice—at your next engagement, ask the sponsor what guidelines apply. If you're in doubt, leave it out. Your most valuable product is yourself. It is foolish to risk diminishing your image and reputation for the sake of a few sales.

10. People Who Know Each Other

Do the members of your audience know each other? Are they part of an ongoing group? If so, a get-acquainted exercise that would loosen up a bunch of strangers may fall very flat. If they know each other, do they have a hierarchical or comradly relationship? If their boss or leader is present, we may want to recognize him or her in some flattering way. After all, the boss usually sets the tone for the group—and is instrumental in seeing that we get invited back to speak again.

Chapter 4
HOW TO PREPARE YOUR INTRODUCER

A good introduction prepares the audience for what is to come. That's its purpose. I like intros that are short, lively, and to the point. Some people who introduce you, however, have their own agendas. They like to talk and, if not checked, will recite everything they know about you—your birthplace, high school, college and graduate degrees, publications, hobbies, family members' names. This means your audience is bored before you open your mouth. The last time I got an overly effusive intro, I tried to turn it into a joke. I thanked the person who introduced me and then said to the audience, "After that introduction, I can hardly wait to hear what I have to say."

You are responsible for your own introduction. If you provide the introducer with a résumé and leave it to his or her devices, it is an invitation to a dull intro. What you may gain in credibility when all your credentials are announced, you lose in audience eagerness when they've been subjected to a dreary recitation of the unnecessary. Tell the introducer what you want said, maybe one important thing about you, and what your topic is. Better yet, write out the introduction, but never let the introducer discuss the topic. That's your job.

A good intro creates eagerness, even a little excitement. It also saves your name for last. Here's a weak intro: "Bill Evans has spent the last ten months in India studying elephants. In that time he learned a lot of interesting things and is here tonight to share them with us." A stronger intro would be: "Tonight we're going to hear some fascinating discoveries about Indian elephants and a few adventure stories from a man who spent the last ten months living with them. Please welcome Bill Evans."

The only good argument I've ever heard for having the introducer repeat your names a few times in the course of the introduction is that it increases the likelihood that people will remember it. This may be true of a small percentage of your audience. Most of your listeners will remember or forget whether they hear it one time or four. What slight edge you gain by having your name repeated, you more than lose in dramatic impact. Some speakers are so conscious of dramatic impact that they won't even let an audience see them until they're introduced. Scott McKain, a superb speaker/entertainer, is one of these. He recommends staying late rather than showing up early to meet people. Keeping the audience in suspense builds anticipation.

If the occasion calls for a few academic, publication or business credentials to enhance your credibility, ask the introducer to refer to you as "our speaker" until the end of the introduction. Your name has more impact if used as the punch word of the introduction and not sooner. A good introducer helps create what I call your "legend." The term derives from spycraft and denotes a persona created by your agency to present to the world. The legend is a story that gives you a personality and a history. Part of an introducer's job is to get the audience on your side by talking about you in a way that 1) distinguishes you from others and 2) prepares the audience to listen to you by giving them a reason or two to like you. If someone the audience knows and trusts tells your story, it greatly increases the warmth of your reception and your listeners' degree of focus when you start your talk.

Like so many lessons, I learned this one the hard way. I failed to tell an introducer what to say about me. It resulted in an inane, single sentence introduction that said nothing about me or my qualifications for speaking on my topic. The seriousness of my omission really came home to me when, after the program, an audience member asked me if I was a licensed psychologist with a relationship counseling practice. Now that I think of it, speech coaching isn't all that different from a counseling practice. I teach people how to connect, only with audiences instead of with intimate partners. Then, too, giving a good speech requires some of the same things necessary for having a good relationship: care, respect and passion.

An introduction that is overly flattering may backfire in another way. If the introducer makes you sound too good to be true—the best this, the greatest that—some audience members may take the attitude, "Oh yeah, well show me. No one can be that good!" This puts needless pressure on you to perform at an unrealistically high level. I love an introduction that has some humor to it, humor at my expense. When the audience sees me laughing, they know before I start that I don't take myself too seriously. That's something I want them to know about me from the get-go.

On occasion, you may have to introduce yourself. This gives you more control but less latitude. Only a fool would not feel foolish listing his or her degrees and achievements. My advice is, stick to the Alcoholics Anonymous outline for story telling: say where you were, where you are, and how you got from there to here. All we want to know about a stranger who's going to address us is: Who are you and what's your story?

Chapter 5
PUTTING A SPEECH TOGETHER

Structure Is Important

A friend of mine who teaches public speaking believes firmly in the Toastmaster formula: tell them what you'll tell them, tell them, then tell them what you told them. It baffled me that he adhered to such a predictable organizational scheme when there are so many more entertaining ways to structure remarks. During one of our discussions, my friend mentioned some research that showed how retention is increased through repetition. The proverbial light went off in my head. No wonder my friend likes the Toastmaster formula. He is an educator and judges the success of a speech on how much of it an audience remembers.

Although I served time as an academician, I come from a show business background. My parents were performers: my mother gave book readings; my father acted in plays. Entertainment was their goal, not retention. The only thing they cared about was if people remembered how much fun they had at the performance. To this day, although I value education, I tend to gauge the success of a presentation by how much fun people have.

My impulse to entertain first, educate second, may have more to do with my personality than upbringing. In a classroom setting, we can test how much people learned from our well organized words. In non-academic settings, we can only hope. Entertainment, on the other hand, has immediate indicators:

> Did people pay attention?
> Did they ask questions?
> Did they eagerly discuss what you said?
> Did they laugh at what you intended as humor?

Since I have a very weak delayed gratification differential—that is to say, I want what I want when I want it—entertainment makes a more convenient goal for me. Only recently have I come to a renewed appreciation of careful structure.

Provide Cues For Your Audience

Audiences like it better if you give them signposts, cues to where you're taking them so that they can follow more easily. A movie like *Belle du Jour*, in which there is no apparent sequence to the events and no clear distinction between real and imagined events, may be interesting as art but would madden an audience that had come out to hear a speech. Not that a speech isn't an art form. It most assuredly is, both in its creation and delivery. It's a combination of essay writing and performance. Yet a speaker whose primary goal is to entertain can actually show an audience an even better time by making it easier for them to grasp the organization of the presentation. People like to be in-the-know, oriented, with the program. To accommodate them is just good manners, a sign of courtesy. If you want them to carry away ideas or information, you greatly enhance your chance of succeeding if you tell them what to listen for.

Elsewhere in this book I advocate beginning

with a personal anecdote. The anecdote—or whatever opening you choose—leads into your topic. You will do well to state the topic in a way that goes beyond the mere title of the speech, which probably appears in a program or announcement, or fell from the lips of the person who introduced you. Let people know why you're talking to them and what you intend for them to learn or do as a result of your efforts. In this regard, it may be better to be blatant than to understate your intent. For better or worse, most people are poor listeners. They don't always get the signpost unless you point it out to them.

I can remember talks I gave that left listeners wondering what my point was—even though I had told them. The trouble was that I had told them so subtly or quickly that it didn't register. Like many beginning speakers, I took too much for granted. What was very clear in my mind was far less clear in the minds of my listeners. I hadn't taken care to articulate the topic and the way points related to it in a simple, direct way.

Another important point to remember is that most people retain things they see better than things they hear. As the deliverer of an idea, you have probably seen that idea in script as well as having thought of it to begin with. You might even have researched it thoroughly. Your audience, on the other hand, only gets to hear it, which means they need to hear it in such a way that it will stick in their minds.

For example, I did a program as part of a leadership seminar. My part was to show how communication is an instrument of leadership and to give some tips on how to be a better communicator. The person who introduced me said that I would focus on one part of leadership, namely communication. I said that I would talk about ways to communicate more effectively so as to lead more effectively.

That was not enough for some members of the audience. Their evaluations made it all too evident that they thought the program was geared toward public speaking as opposed to leadership. The relationship between communication and leadership that the person who introduced me and I thought we had spelled out didn't register with some people.

The next time I did that program, I gave a longer, clearer statement of our purpose. It worked. People then understood the goal and how the various exercises related to it. They participated more enthusiastically, learned more and had more fun.

People will remember how you made them feel long after they've forgotten what you said. Part of how you make them feel has to do with making it easier for them to follow what you say.

Never Read Your Speech

A student in one of my classes got up to give her first presentation and began to read from her notes. Usually I withhold comment until students finish, but reading from notes warrants instant interruption. I asked her to put the notes aside and just tell us her introduction. "If you then can't think of your first point," I added, "you can look at the notes again to refresh your memory, then tell us what it is."

Even this flustered her. She had convinced

herself that without constant reference to the notes she wouldn't know what to say. I asked her what the talk was about. "Selling art," she said. "I help people choose art for their homes and offices."

Already she had an adequate opening.

I then asked why people sought her service.

Without looking at her notes she very articulately told me how people without art training are often insecure about their taste. Her clients were eager to have other people think of them as having good taste.

Another student asked what kind of art she sold the most of.

The speaker beamed and described the paintings of a particular artist. "They're big and bold, full of color and movement. Even though abstract, they convey a sense of life and positive energy. Clients love the way they transform a dull office into a cheerful environment."

By the time another student asked how she decorated her own home, she was on a roll. She said how she had to compromise with her husband, whose taste ran toward the traditional, and even threw in a anecdote about her dog having used a piece of sculpture she planned to show a client as a fire hydrant. The class loved it. She had given a lively, interesting talk without any notes. What it lacked in polish it more than made up for in charm.

How did she do it? Easy. She picked a topic and answered three questions people might have about it—the who, what and where. That's as simple an organizational scheme as there is—and as solid.

Presumably we pick topics we know something about. To give a talk on any topic—

parenting, parachuting, politics, putting, punting or pinochle—all we need do is think of three questions people might have and answer them. If the answers are long, we might get by with two. If short, five questions might be wise.

One good question might center around our personal interest in the topic. When did it begin? How did we learn about the subject? What about it captivates us? Other possible questions could stem from popular misconceptions. What are they? How did they get started?

Still other questions might be: What practical use is there for the subject or activity? Who benefits most? How is it performed? What do people who practice it regard as their greatest challenge? How do they hope to meet the challenge? What kind of people does the subject appeal to most? Why? Who are or were some of its greatest practitioners? What is their legacy?

If you fear that you'll forget the questions, write them on an index card, your wrist, or a flip chart. Even three easy points may be hard to remember if you're nervous. It's all right to look at your notes as long as you look back at your audience before you start to talk. You want to deliver every word to the individuals in your audience, not to your notes. All informative and persuasive presentations are, at base, answers to questions. "What is Greek myth?" "Why is it to everyone's benefit to recycle plastic?" "How will gratuitous acts of courtesy improve your life?" "When did the Incas flourish?" "Where are the best places to look for dinosaur fossils?"

An introduction can be as short as one sentence. "I want to tell you what politics is and how it affects all of us." A closing statement can be equally brief. After all, its main purpose is to signify that the presentation is complete. "To sum up, democracy prospers only when people participate."

There are other ways to organize a speech, and surely more interesting ways to begin than with a simple announcement. A speaker need do no more than relate a topic, answer some questions about it, and thank the audience for the privilege of addressing them to have a complete and, if well done, effective presentation.

How To Compose Your Speech

Lots of ways exist to compose speeches. The way that works best for me is to write down every idea that comes to me about the subject. Since many of these ideas come at unanticipated times, when I'm not sitting at my desk, it's handy to carry a notepad—or just a piece of paper—during all waking hours. We never know when our whimsical muse will visit us, and her cryptic messages can quickly flee if not recorded. The time we waste trying to rethink what spontaneously occurred to us is far greater than that we need to scribble the ideas at their moments of arrival. A short pencil beats a long memory.

When you've assembled some ideas, go through and select those you think are the most important. Decide which ideas are distinct and which are variations of each other. Ask yourself if there's a natural sequence of ideas. Such a sequence might be chronological, developmental (e.g., from problem to solution), geographic (originating one place and moving to others), or logical (progressing from a set of indisputable facts and an agreed upon goal, or premise, to a conclusion).

Think of three ways to begin the presentation. We'll discuss some in the next chapter. Try the alternatives on a friend or two. Get outside input. Ask yourself which you feel most comfortable with and which is the most likely to get your audience's attention and affection.

For a closer, you have as many options as for openers. You can summarize, read a relevant quote, issue a call for action, or tell a story. Make sure your audience knows that you're concluding. That's the primary purpose of a closing. It is a signal to clap.

Stay put while your audience is clapping. They are thanking you for your effort. If you turn your back and head for your seat, you've not reciprocated their gratitude. When people are nice to us, we thank them. It would be rude not to. So thank your audience for thanking you. Hold your ground and smile your pleasure at their response to you. It reinforces the connection you labored to create.

A final note. Write the speech out in its entirety. It forces you to think through every thought to see if it makes sense. A manuscript also gives you something to edit. Editing on paper or a computer is far easier than doing it entirely in your head.

Another reason to write out every word is that it reinforces the ideas in your mind and familiarizes you with your own material. Writing also intensifies your thinking. Creativity is tied to the hands: it's cerebral and manual. We don't experience the full joy of creation when we simply ponder a problem and fasten on a solution. Committing the process to paper (or hard drive) is a large part of the fun. That's why I'm an advocate of, "Don't just think it; ink it."

Just because you've written the speech out doesn't mean you have to memorize it. It's dangerous to memorize your speech. If you forget something, it's much harder to improvise than if you're prepared to deliver it extemporaneously. I once heard a highly paid and, in many ways, a very able speaker say, "Any speech written out word for word doesn't deserve to be given." He then delivered a rambling, disjointed presentation with no discernible point. It had the merit of spontaneity at the cost of coherence. Furthermore, it didn't deserve a tenth of the time it took.

Reinforce Important Points

Back to that old formula: tell them what you'll tell them, tell them, tell them what you told them— with one exception. It's much more powerful if you change the third step to: let the audience tell you what you told them. That way you 1) involve the audience, 2) have them reinforce your message with each other, and 3) give yourself a rest before issuing your closing remarks.

You can let the audience tell you what you've told them by asking individuals to stand and share something they learned and how they intend to use it. You can also ask people to form small groups and prioritize the three or four most important things they got from the program. This leads to discussion of your message and lets people put their own spin on it. That does a lot more for retention—and fun— than your reiterating what you said, even if you word it differently. The best audience is an active audience. Their participation makes them feel good about themselves. When they feel good about themselves, they feel good about you.

Chapter 6
WAYS TO BEGIN

Start Out Lively

Different presentations have different objectives. Different objectives call for different strategies. One strategy remains constant: get the audience's attention at the outset. No matter what kind of speech you give or what you hope its effect on the audience will be, you have only a few seconds to make a first impression. If you don't grab your audience's interest right away, you'll have a formidable task to get it as you move along.

While there are many good ways to open, I know of no better one than the personal anecdote. The people in your audience want to know who you are. Even the most skillful introducer doesn't go very far in telling what you're like as a human being. A personal anecdote both gets people's attention and helps them get to know you. The right anecdote will do even more: make you instantly likeable.

What's the right anecdote? A brief story that is self-effacing, inoffensive and funny. It need not be funny if your subject calls for something solemn. For example, if you want to persuade people to get their wills written or urge their elected representatives to enact tougher punishments for drunk drivers, a sad story may be appropriate. My personal view is that it's still better to save the sad story for a little later, after you've built some rapport, than to lead off with it. A story which is both personal and sad may seem like a plea for sympathy, or worse, self-pitying. You don't want your audience to perceive you as using them as a crying towel.

A story which shows you in a position of vulnerability, as having messed up in some way and learned from it, is a good way to go. Vulnerability is one of our greatest strengths when we allow it to be. People can easily identify with your mistake, embarrassment or fear. They can also relate to what you learned from it. And that lesson can serve as an introduction to—maybe even the whole theme of— your talk.

Another advantage of a personal story is that it's the easiest thing in the world for us to deliver. You don't have to fear you'll forget your opening line. You need only remember what story you want to tell, and the telling will take care of itself. That's because we tell stories about ourselves all the time: what happened at work, at school, at the game, on our vacation, at the store. Each of our lives is a series of anecdotes held together by the thread of individual consciousness.

Be Real

When we tell a story we are far less likely to sound as though we are giving a speech, that is talking *at* people instead of *with* them. The thing audiences want from us more than anything else is authenticity. They are quick to pick up on any phoniness or transparent attempt to win goodwill through flattery or laughter. Even a well-told, genuinely funny joke has the effect of shielding us from them, of substituting amusement for self-revelation and the connection it promotes. Laughter does little to serve rapport unless it either arises out of the immediate situation or we make ourselves the object of the laughter. That's the reason Jack Benny was the finest of all comedians. He gave most of the punch lines to the people around him and allowed himself to be the target of their remarks. It's also the reason this book has no chapter on humor. I've read dozens of humor chapters and articles. None of them tell you how to be funny, only some very obvious ways not to, like don't tell racist, sexist or risqué jokes.

An example of humor arising from the situation occurred during a class of mine at an adult learning center. In order to get paid I had to collect and turn in students' tuition receipts, or green slips. After having asked for the third time that those who had not already given me their green slips please do so, my refrain began to sound like a broken record. Half-way into the class, a pigeon alighted on the ledge of the small room's only window. Since he caught everyone's attention, I turned to him and said, "Excuse me, do you have a green slip?" The remark brought laughter not because it was funny in itself but rather for its spontaneity and the way it related to the situation.

Save Your Thanks until the End

We've all heard presentations that began with a thank you and an announcement of the speaker's happiness and appreciation for the chance to be there. We may have heard it so often that we've begun to think there's no other way to begin. Just as letters begin with a salutation (Dear Mom), we begin to believe that speeches must also begin with the predictable "Thank you for inviting me. It's great to be here," or "A funny thing happened to me today." However sincerely those words or ones like them are spoken, we've become inured to them. They are predictable, and predictability does little to build rapport. That which is fresh, personal, and revelatory creates more rapport in a few minutes than equal time spent on formulaic gratitude, flattery and witty entertainment.

Does that mean we never express gratitude for the privilege of addressing an audience? Of course not. Thanks has its place, and that place is near or at the end of the talk, when you and your audience have a relationship beyond the fact that you're in a room together. Your thanks at the end of your talk is far more likely to sound spontaneous and heartfelt than at the beginning, when it comes across as little more than an obligatory announcement.

How To Organize a Story

A good way to organize the story, if organization is required, is to begin with place and time. For example:

"A few years ago, I was on the last day of a three week trek in Nepal...."
"Last week I was shopping at a hardware store...."
"When I was about ten years old, my friends and I used to swim in a creek near...."
"Until just a month ago I had never ridden a roller coaster. Then...."
In fifth grade I sat behind a girl named Elsie whose pigtails...."

Each of these beginnings sets a stage and invites the listener to participate imaginatively. They create interest. The audience wants to know what will happen and what will it mean. Note: you just start the story. Since it serves as an introduction, it requires none of its own. Getting right into the action is far better than wasting time saying, "I'd like to tell you a story about...."

Next you give the action, introducing just enough detail to help the listeners to visualize what's going on, to make the event or events real. Too little detail is better than too much. The human imagination needs only the barest essentials to set it in motion. Think of the narrative style we find in most Bible stories. Someone goes to a mountain, builds an altar, and returns. Two people argue, one curses the other and departs. A man loves a woman, serves her father seven years for the privilege of marrying her, and collects his bride. Abundant description retards the flow of the story. You offer it not as literature, just an anecdote, a vehicle for telling the audience who you are.

Lastly, you connect the story to the topic of your presentation. The connection can be very tenuous. It's far better to have a good story with a fragile connection to your topic than a humdrum story that fits the topic perfectly. People appreciate and remember good stories for their own sake. They'll find ways to relate it to your main message you may never have dreamed of.

An exercise I like to do in seminars is to have people tell each other personal anecdotes in groups of four or five. After each person tells his or her story, the others suggest topics for which the story could be used as an introduction. Participants are amazed at the multiplicity of meanings their stories have for other people.

Don't worry about making your story conform to fact. Embellish, edit, invent. Tell the story the way things should have happened. You're not writing history; you're creating meaning. Speakers are artists.

I heard a woman give a lively talk on how to be an entrepreneur. Few of her points have stayed with me, but I'll long remember a story she told about an overweight lady who, while making her first sales call, tripped on a porch stair and tore her pantihose, then got her high heel stuck in the grid work of a floor heating duct. The saleslady had to carry on with one shoe off. Topics to which the story could apply are: Expect the Unexpected, Turning Miscues into Assets, Contending with Adversity, How to Sell in Spite of Yourself, There's More to Image Than Image, "Dress for Success" Means More Than You Think.

Start with a Startling Statistic

Another way to begin a talk is with a shocking fact, a startling statement or statistic. "One out of every four women in this room will be sexually assaulted by the time she turns forty." Or: "The National Security Agency has a larger budget than the Central Intelligence Agency and can legally listen to any overseas call you make or receive. They don't even need a warrant." Or: "In the United States over the last 10 years, 6,890 homeless people have starved or frozen to death each year."

These kinds of statements get people's attention. So do questions that force people to think about an issue in a new way. "Who here would not think it cruel if a cosmetic manufacturer took your pet, tortured it in a laboratory, then killed it? Is it any less cruel if the tortured animal is not your pet?" Another example: "If you had reason to believe that your household drinking water were poisoned, would you have it tested? If you knew you had asbestos in your attic, would you try to find out if it posed a cancer threat? Did you know that a deadly gas called radon might be under your house and seeping into it? So why haven't you had your house tested for radon?"

Not only do these kinds of statements or questions get people's attention, they make clear at the outset what your speech is about. One warning: you need to deliver them with just the right tone or you risk coming across as bombastic, using a shock tactic for the sake of shock rather than to make a point. I prefer a calm, low key kind of delivery for this kind of opening. It conveys seriousness without seeming to sermonize. That's much more intense than a tone of indignation or outrage. If indignation and outrage is what you want your audience to feel—and well it might be for many a topic—let those attitudes develop from the facts you provide in the body of your talk. It's almost always better to lead than push.

Start Your Speech with a Quote

An interesting, funny or surprising quote makes a strong opening. "All men should strive to learn before they die, what they are running from, and to, and why." Those lines of James Thurber's could begin a talk on our search for meaning in life or the need to acknowledge to ourselves both our aspirations and fears. Friedrich Nietzsche's aphorism, "A very popular error: having the courage of one's convictions. Rather it is a matter of having courage for an attack on one's convictions!" could serve as an opening for a discussion of dogmatism, intellectual integrity, or the meaning of courage in the realm of ideas.

Anthologies of quotes abound. The best known is Bartlett's *Book of Familiar Quotations*, with over 1,000 entries. At the end of this book, I've given you some favorite quotes I've encountered in my own reading.

Pose a Question

Speakers often begin with a question. It works if the question is sincere. A disingenuous question, on the other hand, makes you look manipulative. "How many of you would like to have financial independence?" "Would any of the overweight people in the room like to lose ten pounds a week without having to give up their favorite food?" These kind of no-brainer questions are transparent devices to get people saying "yes." As such, they are an affront to the intelligence of an audience and have no place in the repertoire of any speaker other than a crude salesperson.

A few weeks ago, a stock broker tried to telemarket me with questions to which I knew that he knew the answers. I called him on it. I asked why he was asking what he already knew. He was stuck for an answer. Maybe he learned something from our brief exchange.

Rhetorical questions are useful to get people thinking. Rather than asking them in a way that invites a verbal response, just preface them with "Ask yourself...." Some speakers use this means to help the audience formulate, even visualize, the problem the speaker intends to address. If you can think of fresh questions or at least a fresh way to phrase old questions, you'll prompt more mental activity on your listeners' part.

I find that questions work better after the audience has had time to warm up to me. Even good-natured questioning can come across as interrogation if the people to whom the questions are addressed aren't quite comfortable with the questioner yet. If you open with a question, give thought to cueing a few members of the audience in advance. That will make them feel like part of the show and assure you of a response. To have a question met with silence is always a downer, unless that's what you intend. I remember beginning a talk on persuasion by asking who in the audience had never given a persuasive speech. Of course, no hands went up. "Just what I thought," I said. "We all give persuasive speeches all the time—to our friends, kids, colleagues, clients, and mates. So let's look at some ways we can become better persuaders." It worked all right, but in retrospect, I think an anecdote would have worked better.

Chapter 7
DELIVERY

Be Authentic
A great deal of literature exists on the techniques of effective public speaking. What we sometimes lose sight of in our eagerness to embrace the "right" techniques is that they all serve a greater goal. That goal is authenticity. Effectiveness begins and ends with authenticity, what we more often call being real. No amount of cleverness, of mere technique gets us to the summit of communication, that point at which dialogue becomes a secular sacrament, something that touches people at a deep level, brings them closer to each other and to, whatever they may call it, a larger reality.

Several years ago I heard Daniel Schorr, the National Public Radio news analyst, give a talk in which he described his initial transition from radio to television. The head of the broadcasting company called him in, sat him down and said this. "Listen, Dan, I know you're nervous, but don't worry. In TV there's only one important thing: sincerity. If you can fake that, you'll have no problem."

This somewhat cynical remark points up an important fact. Audiences demand sincerity. They want to know that the speaker not only believes what he or she says but also has an emotional connection to the content. Truth in advertising laws are an outgrowth of the public's insistence on credibility on the part of those who address us. We have neither time nor the stomach to listen to messages we can't believe. Not just advertisers but politicians are held to a higher standard of credibility than formerly, though still not a high enough one to satisfy some of us.

A speaker has an ethical responsibility to speak the truth. In order for that truth to meet with the best possible reception, the speaker needs to come across as truthful, sincere, authentic, real. No one can tell us how to be sincere. Either we are or we aren't. If we are, there are things we can do to reinforce and demonstrate it.

Seven Tips for Conveying Sincerity

1. Give accurate and adequate information.

Let your listeners make their own informed, reasoned decisions. Your appeals for cooperation will fall on more receptive ears if your audience feels that you respect their intelligence and allow them to decide matters for themselves.

People embrace points of view far more strongly if they arrive at them on their own. Logic is as integral to persuasion as information, and the best logic is the logic your audience comes up with for itself on the basis of information you provide. Laboring a point which any reasonable person can easily grasp may do more harm than good. The best argument is one in which you present the relevant information in such a way that the audience is led by their own reasoning to the conclusion you want.

A student of mine gave an in-class speech in which he described the hazards of wearing jewelry in a machine shop. After relating some horrifying stories of what happened to people whose ring or necklace got caught in a power tool, he closed with the admonition to remove any metal adornments from one's body before using any kind of power tool. The admonition was totally unnecessary. He had more than made his point with the information and examples he provided. By including a superfluous admonition, he risked insulting the intelligence of his listeners and seemed to talk down to them.

Ethics and practicality demand that we give accurate and adequate information. No matter how noble the cause at hand, when we distort or withhold relevant data that may be injurious to the position we espouse, we cease to be a role model and become a mere manipulator. Once our audience perceives that we have skewed or hidden information, we lose our credibility.

A wise alternative to selective revelation of facts is to admit information that runs counter to your argument and try to undercut its effect. If you can't undercut its effect, then a good strategy is to show how its importance is outweighed by countervailing information and argument. For example, suppose you are speaking on behalf of abolishing the death penalty. An irrefutable argument of the other side is that capital punishment deters forever at least one criminal, namely the executed person, from committing another crime. The only sensible way to deal with this argument is to acknowledge its validity and present reasons that you believe carry more weight and incline us toward the abolition of the death penalty.

2. Listen.

"How does a speaker listen?" you ask. We've already talked about one way: arrive early and engage audience members in conversation. Another is to pay close attention to questions you get after your presentation, whether in a public question-and-answer period or informal conversation. The questions can help you identify parts of your talk that you need to clarify, amplify, or edit. They also give clues as to how a shift of focus would make the talk more relevant to similar audiences.

I gave a speech to a group of Rotarians, all but two of whom were men. The topic was the parallels between a good speech and a good personal relationship, especially in marriage. It drew a lot of questions about speaking technique but none about running a relationship. Part of that reason may have been that I have a far better track record in the former than the latter. A more likely reason might be that the gentlemen present wanted to know things that could help them as businessmen rather than as husbands. In future talks to Rotarians, I concentrated on what they wanted to hear rather than what I thought was important for any past, present or future married person to hear.

We can also listen with our eyes—while we are speaking. If half the audience looks befuddled, you want to restate whatever befuddled them. Reword it to make the meaning clearer. You may even stop and ask someone to tell you what is unclear. Likewise, if people fail to laugh at what you intended as a humorous story or line, you may want to rephrase it on the spot, make a mental note to drop it from future presentations, or add some self-deprecating remark like, "I've had quieter audiences but always at an earlier mass."

3. Organize, edit, practice.

Treat a speech as an art form, a gift of your labor to others. Respect your audience—all audiences. They honor us with their presence. As speakers, we have an obligation to reward them with the best effort we are capable of giving.

You wouldn't invite friends to dinner and serve them a half-cooked meal to which you gave no thought until five minutes before their arrival. You'd think about food that would please them, perhaps ask in advance if there are foods they'd prefer not to eat, if they have wine preferences, calorie concerns. Then you'd carefully plan a meal that not only tasted delicious but looked good on the table. You'd order the courses so as to build up to the main course. Maybe you'd have background music, incense, a floral centerpiece. You'd make the meal an event, and you'd do it through planning and loving preparation. If you were unsure of the best way to fix one or more of the dishes, you'd do a trial ahead of time to see how it tasted and if there was a way to improve it. Your guests would know the effort you put into the meal, the love of your craft and of them you demonstrated.

Planning a speech is very much the same. When we plan with love, the audience knows it, just as it would note our indifference if we merely rambled through some hastily assembled, uncritically edited notes.

The spoken word differs from the written. If you hand someone a six-page report, he or she can skip around, recheck something on page two while reading page five, reorganize the contents in his or her own way. The spoken word, however, is in the air but a second, then gone. We retrieve it only via audio or video tape. Therefore, its position in the whole is much more critical. The debate over whether your most important point is better put first or last may continue indefinitely. One thing is sure; both sides agree that the position of points, be they points of information or argument, is very important. A speaker ignores organization at his peril and to the dismay of his audience.

I counsel clients to listen to themselves on tape. It is a real ear opener. They notice things they would not otherwise be aware of. They hear what I mean when I remark on a misplaced emphasis, a repetitive vocal pattern, the need for a strategic pause. If time permits, I give them a video of a practice run so that they can see their gestures, body language and facial expressions, then make a reasoned decision about what to change and what not. There's no substitute for preparation.

4. Stay conversational.

Talk with people, not at them. You never want to sound like one of those self-righteous, self-important congresspersons we see on the news blustering from the podium of the House or Senate (unless, of course, you are one of them). Your audience will find you more credible if you talk to them as friends, people you're deeply pleased to share some ideas with. Audiences appreciate poise and confidence in a speaker. They also respond warmly to the speaker who conveys a sense that he or she is just one of them who temporarily occupies the role of speaker.

5. Eschew the podium.

You may feel safer behind a podium, but what you gain in "safety" you more than lose in accessibility. Any physical barrier (a chair, table, podium, anything) between you and your audience can become a psychological barrier—even your arms crossed over your chest.

In the speaking profession, the term for making yourself physically accessible to your audience is, "Share your body." It has two meanings: let nothing come between you and your listeners and use your body as an instrument of communication. A podium severely limits what you can do with your body to complement your words. The natural tendency is to rest your hands on the top of the podium and never lift them except to shuffle notes. So unless you have an auditorium full of people, and the only microphone is permanently bolted to the podium, get out in front of it where your audience can see all of you.

6. Smile often.

We all respond favorably to smiles. A smile is a universal sign of warmth and regard. When smiling it's practically impossible to utter words in anything but a conversational way. If you have a smile on your face, you'll be far less likely to engage in waving or wagging your finger. A wagged finger connotes moral superiority, makes the wagger look like an elementary school principal who has just caught you in the lavatory doing something naughty. We're all familiar with a far more infamous finger gesture, one performed with the middle rather than index finger. Yet the notorious middle finger gesture at least has the merit of being a spontaneous expression of emotion, the kind of emotion a finger-wagger may provoke.

You can also do yourself and your audience a favor by eliminating words such as "ought", "should", and "must". There are always ways to communicate the idea of necessity, or just ethical good sense without resorting to language we associate with authority, either legal or ecclesiastical.

7. Eye contact goes along with listening.

These are the two most powerful tools you have as a communicator. When you make a presentation, speak every word to someone while you look him or her in the eyes. How sincere do you find a speaker who talks to the wall, ceiling or floor, out a window or to his or her notes? How likely are you to trust a salesperson who keeps looking away from you? Eyes are windows to the soul. Let people look into your eyes by looking into theirs. Eye contact can't guarantee that you'll appear sincere, but the absence of eye contact almost guarantees that an audience will suspect you lack sincerity.

If you want to experience the power of eye contact, try this exercise. Sit with someone you know well or have just met and face each other with your knees almost touching. Put your hands on your thighs and give each other one minute of sustained eye contact without smiling, nodding or otherwise using body language or facial expression to reassure each other. Just look at your partner and be with him or her. It's not a staring contest. You can blink.

The idea is to experience the subtle yet palpable power of pure eye contact without trappings. You may feel uncomfortable, even threatened, or you may feel a closeness beyond what words and smiles produce. In any case, you'll very likely get an appreciation of the power of eye contact. I sometimes use this exercise in seminars. Very often people will tell me that it was both the hardest and most worthwhile thing they did the whole day.

You may not have a chance to give every person their full measure of eye contact with a large audience. Yet if you speak every word to someone, you'll have a connection to other members of the audience. The audience knows when you're connected to someone or talking to the wall. That's one of the main bases on which they'll assess your sincerity, if only unconsciously,

A phenomenon that works in your favor is that every member of your audience has a psychic connection to the person on either side. That means if you look at a person seated between two others, the other two are included by virtue of the energetic field that rings them. I was long aware of this three-for-one benefit derived from eye contact but didn't understand what lay behind it until a psychologist in one of my classes explained it.

How long do you look at one person before moving on to another? At least five seconds, otherwise the eye contact is so transient that it barely registers. A really good tactic is to complete an entire thought, or at least sentence, with your eyes on the same person, then start and complete your next thought with someone else. Between thoughts is a natural place to pause and shift your eyes to another person.

As is the case with most delivery techniques, varying your eye contact strengthens your total impact. For example, when you finish a thought while looking at a person, don't immediately look away. Let your eyes stay with him or her for another few seconds while the thought sinks in. When you do look away, instead of always looking at someone on the other side of the room, now and then speak your next thought to someone very close to the person you just looked at.

If you need to consult your notes, do so, but don't keep talking while you do. Just stop and find your place. Your audience understands and will wait for you.

It's important to think about what you are saying *while* you're saying it. You can't focus on your words and something else—your notes, the clock, who walked in late—at the same time. That's why memorizing a speech is dangerous. You know it so well that you tend to think about the next sentence before you've finished speaking the one you're in the middle of. I call it mind-ahead-of-mouth syndrome. Your audience will pick up on the disconnection between your words and thought and perceive you as insincere.

The best delivery is natural delivery. If people perceive that you are performing, they'll judge you by performance standards. If they see you as being natural, they'll credit you for it. So be yourself, just more so, and you're sure to shine.

Chapter 8
YOUR VOICE

Your vocal cords are your primary tool. How much resonance they produce without special conditioning is determined largely by your genes. James Earl Jones came into the world with the right stuff for a special voice, one of enormous depth and richness. Few of us will ever come close to sounding the way he does. Don't despair. Whatever our present voice quality, we can improve it through training.

Most of us are lazy in our speech habits. We formulate sound in our heads and run it through our nasal cavity, or we talk from the throat, creating tight, squeezed sounds. The secret to voice improvement is deep breathing. We can get a more pleasing, powerful sound when we bring air up from our abdomen. We need only practice deep, diaphragmatic breathing to do this. Exhale hard to clear your lungs. Take a full, deep, slow breath, then concentrate on letting your breath come from the depths of your abdomen while you speak. You'll hear and feel the difference.

It takes most of us about twenty-one days to form a new habit. Make it a point for three weeks to practice deep breathing while making a variety of sounds—all from your diaphragm. I like to do it while doing something else, usually driving or bathing. It doesn't take time away from some "productive" activity that way, and I remember to practice.

What vocal exercises you do are far less important than that you do them regularly. I've found vowel work to be the most useful for me. I go through the vowels, doing them first quickly (ee, ee), then slowly (oooooh). Since my "natural" voice is too nasal for my taste, I concentrate on lowering the sounds. "Aah" sounds are my favorite, so I make much use of the "ong" exercise. Simply repeat King Kong, Ding Dong, Bing Bong a few times. With each phrase try to make the "ong" sound fuller, deeper and more resonant.

Before making a presentation, warm up your vocal chords the way an athlete stretches and warms up his or her muscles before an event. In addition to the breathing and vocalizations just described, I like to massage my mandible, then move it as far as possible in every direction with my facial muscles. I don't know how much difference that makes in the sound of my voice, but it loosens my jaw and makes me feel better prepared.

Another good idea is to lay off milk and flour products for four to six hours before you speak. Both create mucous which contributes to nasality. I don't miss pizza and milkshake before performing, but I hate having to go so long without chocolate.

Remember, your voice conveys confidence more than any other vehicle. It carries your emotional body and is the only part of you that actually enters the bodies of your listeners. A wavering voice reveals an unsteady psyche. If you are nervous pretend you're calm. It works. Fritz Perles, the inventor of Gestalt therapy, said, "Fear is excitement without breath." So breathe deep and be grateful for your excitement. It's contagious!

Chapter 9
PAUSE POWER

Because our voice is our most important tool, we sometimes forget that there are moments to stop speaking. Silence, when well timed, is a very effective communication device. Some situations just plain call for a second or more of silence.

1. When you build to the climax of your presentation and announce, "And now I'll tell you the single most important thing you can do to increase your sales (or health, happiness, peace of mind, or first-serve percentage)," ...... pause. That pause increases suspense and lends emphasis to what follows. In addition, dramatic pauses add flavor, interest and impact to any speech.

2. When you've just made an important point or told a story that gets laughs, tears or looks of astonishment, pause and let the effect sink in. Your audience wants a moment to savor the pleasure or poignant experience you've just given them. If you fail to allow them that moment, you get in your own way by interrupting the very effect you labored to create. We don't remember a lot of what we hear; we long recall how what we heard made us feel.

3. Pause when you shift gears. The shift may be a change of subject or just another point you want to make about the same subject. A pause is

the most natural way to signify that you are about to begin what, if you were writing, would be a new paragraph or fresh heading. To make the transition more emphatic, take a few steps to one side or the other.

An officer of the Colorado AIDS Project sought my help on his acceptance speech for an award at a banquet in his honor. He thanked some colleagues by name and, in the same breath, his parents, who were coming from afar. I suggested pausing before mentioning his parents to distinguish them from the others, then say: "...and thanks to two very special people, who came all the way from Iowa to be with us tonight...my mother and father." We practiced the lines seven times, and all seven times they moved me to tears.

4. Pause when you want to create the impression of greater spontaneity. This is especially useful for speakers who talk fast and have so much control of their material that the presentation appears canned. An occasional pause that makes it look as though you're searching for just the right word does a lot to overcome the mechanical effect that can come from being overly familiar with your material. Better to look a little lost now and then than for everything to appear too easy. Facility can get in the way of sincerity.

At a presidential debate in 1992, George Bush and Ross Perot spat out their answers to questions from the live audience without a second's hesitation. Bill Clinton, on the other hand, paused a few seconds before responding. He looked as though he were hearing the question for the first time (very improbable!) and wanted to think about it before he answered. Whether planned or not, it was a brilliant device that made him look more sincere than his programmed opponents.

More and more, audiences expect customization. Even if you don't create a brand new presentation for every group you address, at least make it look as though part of your program is a new thing. One good way to do that is to deliver it the way you would if it were the first time. Hunt for a phrase; grope for a word. Pause to think.

5. Pause when you relinquish control, such as when you wait for a question from the audience or pose one to them. You always give up control when you conclude, so instead of sprinting to your seat when you finish, or blurting a "thank you" on the heel of your final syllable, pause for a few seconds. Then, say "thank you" or just take a step back and bow your head to let everyone know you're done. Of course if you've created a good last line, everyone will know you're done. Still, the pause gives the close a little punch.

You don't have to give a speech to practice pausing. Next time you talk to anyone, even on the phone, try pausing after an important point or before answering a question and see how it feels. I bet you'll have a sense of exerting more control over the flow of words from your mouth, of orchestrating your part of the dialogue. Can you imagine a symphony without periodic pauses? Orchestrate your talks as though they were pieces of music and you'll pluck your audience's heartstrings.

Chapter 10
HANDLING NERVOUSNESS

Some Nervousness Is Natural

Nervousness, within limits, is our ally. It shows that we're excited, that we care about our presentation, that we are aware of the importance of how our audience regards us. Nervousness that ties us in knots and paralyzes our brain is no fun. There are two ways to avoid the kind of nervousness that debilitates you: mental activities and physical activities.

Preparation

The foremost mental activity is preparation. As one speaker I know likes to put it, "To make yourself immune from debilitating nervousness, do these three things: prepare, prepare, and prepare." While thorough preparation—organizing, editing, and practicing—doesn't guarantee that we won't be nervous, little or no preparing invites nervousness. An unprepared speaker who isn't nervous simply fails to grasp the importance of his or her task.

Preparation can come from different motives. If our objective is simply to avoid making a fool of ourselves, we tend to regard preparation as work, even drudgery. As a result, we do as little as we think we can get away with. On the other hand, if we think of our speech as a gift to our audience, preparation becomes fun. We prepare our speech with anticipation. Our focus is on how much we can give to our audience, much as it is when we shop for or make something that will please someone we love.

All of us have been the recipients of meals prepared with extraordinary care and love. We recognize the effort that went into every aspect of the meal—the order of the courses, how the table looked, and, of course, the taste. The delicious taste is itself the result of scrupulous attention to seasoning, timing, and testing. The meal becomes an event that nourishes us on several levels—aesthetic, social, and gustatory. For some people, food preparation is their primary way of expressing love. (This idea is wonderfully developed in the Mexican film *Like Water for Chocolate*.)

A speech is also a way of expressing love, of showing people we care enough about them to organize, edit and practice a presentation until we can think of nothing more to do to improve it. The reward for this effort is knowing that we've given our utmost and having other people know it, too.

An ancillary benefit is that by focusing on our audience and our regard for them, we cut through our self-consciousness. As Mary Baker Eddy said, "Right motives give pinions to thought and strength and freedom to speech and action."

Breathing

OK, you say, but all this is pretty cerebral. What can I do, if after hours of prep, I'm still uncomfortably nervous when it comes to give my speech? One answer is so old it has passed from esoteric technique to conventional wisdom. Deep breathing. Sit or lie down somewhere, shut your eyes and take a deep breath. Let it out slowly. Try to focus your mind on nothing but the inhalation and exhalation. Feel the air fill your lungs, then exit them. When we concentrate on any action we normally perform automatically and without thought, it has a calming effect. Deep breathing also pushes more oxygen into our blood, which in itself relaxes us. I find that just one minute of deep, slow breathing calms me as much as several minutes of jogging. Breathing has the added advantage of not making you perspire, one of the last things you want to do before you've even started your talk.

Breathing has proved so effective for me that after taking my place in front of an audience, I take a few deep breaths while looking around at the people seated before me. It gives the audience a chance to get focused and lets me establish eye contact with at least a few of them. Usually I can tell at a glance which ones will be sources of energy for me, people who will support me with their attentiveness and nourish me with their smiles. Speaking is about rapport and the rapport can start before you utter a word. Eye contact by itself is enough to establish trust, to create a connection.

Another surefire technique to help your relax is to lock your fingers in front of you with your elbows extended, take a deep breath, then force it out as hard as you can while pulling outward against your locked fingers. You may even want to visualize your nervousness going out with your exhalations.

Exercise
Exercise, in moderation, can both banish nerves and raise your energy. Some speakers like to do yoga before taking the platform. Others prefer a brisk walk around the block. Both are effective. You

can develop your own routine. It doesn't matter so much what you do—breathing, yoga, calisthenics, walking, limb shaking, stretching, or some combination—so long as it works for you. Return to it again and again. The confidence you'll gain in the routine will translate into confidence on the platform. Remember this formula: MC=LS. More circulation equals less stress.

Of course, the day may come when an unforeseen event interrupts your routine. On a day I was to give a talk to a group that meets very early in the morning, my car wouldn't start. In the two years I had owned it, it had never misbehaved before. I thought that my nervousness might be causing me to step on the throttle a different way from usual and flood the thing. This made me even more nervous. My hours of speech preparation wouldn't start the car, and I couldn't give it breathing lessons.

Rather than call a cab and risk being catatonic with panic by the time it arrived, or waking a neighbor and begging to borrow a car, I jumped on my bike and headed for the meeting place. As I pedaled through the dark and cold, it occurred to me that my car's flaky behavior was a blessing. Instead of sitting behind the wheel doing next to nothing, I was active. The exercise and wind in my face felt good. By the time I reached my destination I was almost calm, yet energized. My often pallid complexion probably had a faint rose tint to it. I actually felt thankful for my car not having started— and even more thankful that the meeting place was within bike range.

Chapter 11
MAKING IMPORTANT POINTS:
WAYS TO GAIN EMPHASIS

The inexperienced speaker tends to give emphasis to a word or words in one way only: by raising vocal volume. That works but it's only one way to give a word or phrase emphasis. The fact is, any change of volume or pitch grabs the audience's auditory attention and creates an emphasis. For maximum impact, a good speaker finds different ways to emphasize things. That lends variety to the talk and makes it much more fun to plan.

For example, instead of just speaking louder, you can speak softer. Consider this sentence, which might be found in a talk that favors giving federal judges leeway in sentencing: "What Americans want from federal sentencing procedures—and all facets of their government—is reason, fairness, and flexibility." Since flexibility is the point most at issue in the argument of the talk, it gets the honored position of last word in the sentence. To give it further emphasis, the speaker might increase his volume slightly on "reason," a little more on "fairness," and even more on "flexibility." Equally effective, or maybe even more, would be to increase the volume on the first two qualities, then lower his volume for the third.

Since "flexibility" has five syllables, you could utter the word as though it were a slinky toy, raising the pitch slightly for "flex," a little more for "i," even more for "bil," then let it drop on the last two syllables. That makes the word sound like what it describes. Speaking the word more slowly, dragging it out a bit, gives it even more emphasis. Any word spoken more slowly than others gains emphasis from the change.

Another way to gain emphasis is to reduce the pace. The sudden slow-down adds intensity as does a pause just before you speak a word. Consider this sentence. "Our Founding Fathers made very clear that all of us have certain inalienable rights: life, liberty, and the pursuit of happiness." Where the emphasis falls is up to the speaker. If his main point is that the rights under discussion originated not with some obscure professor of political science but with our Founding Fathers, then those are the words he'll highlight. If it is the irrevocability of the rights he wants to stress, then "inalienable" gets the emphasis. If one or more of the rights is his focus, then he underlines them.

Now ask yourself this. For each of those alternatives, how would you choose to make the emphasis? Would you raise or lower your voice, slow down and stretch the word or words out, pause before the key word or words, or some combination?

I find this kind of self questioning one of the most fun parts of planning a presentation. It both forces me to think about the relative importance of points in the talk and gives me a chance to direct my own performance. It's also a way of demonstrating care for the audience through attention to detail. A really good speaker does everything he can to make his message lively, interesting and entertaining.

Chapter 12
YOUR BODY

Body Language Speaks Louder than Words

As an expressive medium, your body is as important as your voice. It may even be more important, according to an often-quoted piece of research, because the visual impression you make counts for more of your overall effectiveness than how you sound.

I think the voice is more important simply because it's possible to make a presentation with voice alone. Unless you're a mime or signer, you'd be hard put to deliver a "speech" without use of your voice. Which is the more important, voice or body, really isn't worth debating. Good presenters get the most out of both.

We give and receive nonverbal cues all the time. Gerry Spence, the renowned trial attorney and author of *How to Argue and Win Every Time*, says, "Body language is words heard with the eyes." The way we move reveals more about us than what we say. If our physical actions aren't congruent with our words, we appear insincere. How readily would you believe someone who said he was excited about an idea or discovery if he had his hands in his pockets and slumped when he said it?

Our posture and gestures, movements and facial expressions can either reinforce or belie our words. A description of action requires body movement in the same way talk of happiness calls for a smile. In short, we speak with our whole person. Audiences judge us on our movement as surely as they do on our voice. They visually see us before they hear us. And when our last syllable has vanished from their ears, they still see us.

The most fundamental goal of any presentation is communication. Whatever our topic or intent— entertain, motivate, inform, persuade—we have to communicate. The most important thing we communicate is ourselves. Are we prepared, enthusiastic, sincere? These are things our audience rightfully demands of us. What we do with our body goes a long way toward showing that we've done our homework, researched and rehearsed, and that we mean what we say. If an audience has to chose between believing what they hear or what they see, they will trust their eyes over their ears. That is because we all know intuitively that body language rarely lies, while words can mislead. Visually, we give ourselves away. People pick up on subtle signals that speak loudly about our state of mind, forthrightness, pleasure with what we're doing, conviction, and concern for our listeners.

Our body language also gives insight into our nervousness. Audiences are forgiving of nervousness, except in well-known, seasoned professionals who command high fees and of whom they have enormous expectations. We speakers feel better about ourselves if we at least appear relaxed. Getting our bodies to send the message "I'm relaxed and in control" helps us to feel just that way. It's a case of matter over mind, of physical behavior creating empathy, and empathy, the ability to imaginatively enter another person's feelings, is crucial to communication. It goes beyond mere transfer of neutral information, such as the price of potatoes. Our audience can feel whether or not we empathize with them.

Relax Yourself To Relax Your Listeners

When we appear relaxed, we relax our listeners. When we appear confident, we inspire confidence. When we smile, we get smiles in return. When we convey sincerity, people reward us with their trust. Our body language is the most important way we communicate these qualities. It reveals our attitudes as nothing else can.

Beyond providing a gauge of our feelings, body movement makes our presentations more interesting. Action is inherently more interesting than stasis. One need not move a lot. Some speakers do very well simply turning their upper body from time to time so as to face different parts of the audience. Others walk around the room. The fact that we move is more important than how far we move. Movement need not be exaggerated to catch our eye. Think how much attention we squander on insignificant movements every day: a person enters or exits the room; a car drives by; someone drops something.

Movement also aids memory. Very often we associate words with where we heard them, with their visual environment. Anyone old enough to remember the assassination of President Kennedy remembers where he was and what he was doing when the news reached him.

Visual memories stay with us longer than auditory ones. If we can tie a verbal message to an action, our audience will likely have a longer recall of it. We create those visual memories with body movement: gestures, facial expressions, purposeful strides.

When I speak, even informally to a class, I can feel my adrenaline pumping. Communicating is an exciting activity. Just writing these words energizes me. After an evening presentation, I have to take a walk and watch television for a while just to calm down before I go to bed.

A natural way to deal with the nervous excitement we feel in front of a group is to move about. It gives us an outlet for our energy and makes it less likely that we'll lapse into some unconscious mannerism that distracts the audience. Buttoning and unbuttoning one's suit coat is a common example, as is playing with something in one's hand, such as notes or a marker. Movement relieves tension in the speaker, but unless it's effective movement related to the verbal message, it can create tension in the audience. Our bodies send messages in spite of us. It's our job to make sure they send the messages we intend.

Movement Adds Interest

We can use body movement to punctuate a transition or exclamation in our speech. A good way to signal a change of subject or simply another point is to move, if not your whole body, at least part of it. A step forward or forward thrust of an arm lends emphasis to whatever word or words accompany it. Of course, we want our voice to cooperate with the gesture, lest the latter seem contrived or phony.

Another splendid opportunity for movement is when we tell a story in which we change characters. For each character, have a different place. Move to that place and, if appropriate, adopt a different posture to speak that character's lines. Not only does this dissipate your nervous energy, it makes your story much easier and more fun for your audience to follow.

Sam Horn, the author of *Tongue Fu*, has lots of anecdotes in her programs. She is masterful at acting them out, sometimes running across the stage to show what a character did. After watching her perform, I made sure to put lots more physical action into my stories.

The best way to work on body movement is to see yourself in action—either through the eyes of a trusted critic or on video. When I looked at a video of a recent program, I caught myself licking my lips between thoughts. Natural as the gesture may have been (at least to me), it may have looked foolish to the audience. It certainly was unnecessary. You don't have to do something as blatant as jangle the keys in your pocket or fiddle with a piece of jewelry to distract the audience. Any unconscious action that isn't related to your message is a potential distraction. Swaying, pacing, shifting your weight from one foot to the other are common examples of counter-productive body movement. When you eliminate such actions, you give your message—and yourself—a better chance to succeed.

The way to attack a distracting action is simple. Once you become aware of it, make a conscious effort not to do it. If you can find a positive habit to substitute for the offending one, your job will be much easier.

Exaggerate Movements for Large Audiences

The larger our audience the more sweeping our gestures should be. What will seem overly dramatic to a group of ten might be just right for a fifty-person audience. It is also wise to make your facial expressions more extreme for a larger audience. People have to see you from a greater distance, so everything you do, even your stride, needs to be enlarged.

Things appear smaller at a distance. That's why outdoor wildlife sculpture is usually twenty percent larger than life size. From a distance it appears life size. We do well to emulate sculptors in this regard and exaggerate our body movement for the sake of the listener/viewers in the back of the room. To employ exaggeration and still appear natural and conversational may take a little practice, but it is a goal eminently worth attaining.

Since our bodies reflect our attitude, confidence level and self-esteem, our posture plays a vital role in communication. When you take the platform, move in a lively fashion. Demonstrate that you are alert and eager. Once in front of your audience, stand straight. The straighter we stand, the more in charge of ourselves and the situation we appear.

Good posture also facilitates proper breathing, the kind of breathing from the diaphragm we talked about in connection with voice control. Keep your feet about shoulder distance apart with your knees straight but not locked. Distribute your weight equally between your legs. This will keep you upright and balanced. Hold your chin up and relax your shoulders. Take a few deep breaths and feel yourself expand into the space around you. Let your spirit and strength flow into every part of the room, even if it's a huge auditorium. Now you're in command. Your audience sees it, and you feel it.

Gestures Can Aid or Distract

Gestures seem as though they'd be the easiest kind of body language to master. After all, we all use them in normal conversation without even thinking about what we're doing. The problem is that normal conversation is less sustained than even an informal presentation. We also observe presentations from a greater distance; therefore we see more of what a speaker is doing with his hands.

Often speakers just don't seem to know what to do with their hands. Some cross them in front of themselves, which makes them look guarded. Others put them behind themselves, which appears overly casual, as does the familiar hands in pockets stance. All of these positions have the disadvantage of making it hard to use your hands easily. If you had to bring your hand from behind you or out of your pocket every time you want to use a hand gesture, it would distract your audience. A good place for your hands is either relaxed at your sides or in front of you, fingertips lightly touching. In either of these positions, your hands are at the ready.

I prefer to hold my hands in front of my chest. The most natural gestures occur between the waist and chin. If that's where my hands already are, they don't have to go far to accomplish a gesture. Hands held in front of the chest are itself a gesture of thoughtfulness. When I'm not using my hands to make or reinforce a point, I like them to suggest that I'm thinking, either while words spill from my mouth or during a pause. Since all gestures should be purposeful, why not have even your "non-gestures" serve a purpose.

Gestures are powerful nonverbal communicators. Think about sign language, in which hand and finger movements are used to do the job of spoken language. As a baseball player would not consider using a bat only half as thick as that which the rules allow, a good speaker does not deprive himself of such a potent tool as his hands.

You can use your hands to dramatize your words, to help paint a picture. You can gesture how big or how little something is, whether it's round, square or triangular shaped, its height, length and location. These are all perfect opportunities for gestural descriptions. So are handing or taking something, waving or beckoning, rejecting or accepting.

We also use gestures to emphasize points. Any forward thrust of a hand, open or closed, lends emphasis to the word it accompanies. An invitation to the audience to respond gets reinforcement from outstretched, open hands moving toward your body. In a large room, the people in back may not see your features clearly. Gestures become even more important in such a situation to cue the audience as to your meaning and intent. If you want people to raise their hands, stand up, sit back down, or just clap, you can convey these requests with your words *and* gestures.

I reserve gestures above shoulder level to designate either enormous height, surprise, exasperation or exultation. Dramatic points call for dramatic gestures. A dramatic gesture for less than a dramatic point is overkill. Gestures below the waist

I save for indications of shortness. For example, "The leprechaun was no higher than my knee." Bringing the hand down abruptly suggests conclusiveness, as in "And that was the end!" An open hand held up toward the audience can signify rejection or a pause or stop.

Probably no two people gesture exactly alike, and that's as it should be. We're all different and our speaking styles are extensions of our unique personalities. No matter what our speaking style is, some guidelines apply to all gestures. They should feel genuine and spontaneous. Any attempt to adopt another person's gestures will appear insincere.

One gesture that is particularly effective is a slow, sweeping movement of the hand away from the body. One of America's finest speech coaches, Max Dixon, recommends using it early in any talk. It simultaneously conveys inclusion and expansiveness, strength and breadth. Try it next time you talk to anyone, even on the phone, and observe how it makes you feel and sound.

Focus on What You're Saying

Think about your words, not your hands. When you focus on your message it helps you to keep your gestures natural rather than staged. Let your hands range freely in sync with your feelings. This will ensure that your gestures occur at the right time. A gesture made a little too early or late distracts from rather than reinforces your message. A mistimed hand movement is like a mistimed tennis stroke: the ball goes the wrong way. Just as bad is a half-hearted gesture, one that lacks conviction and gives the message that the speaker doesn't really identify with his words or is unsure of himself as a person. That's the next to last thing you want your audience to think. The last, of course, is that you're lying.

Fluidity

A relaxed body builds trust. "Rigidity militates against rapport," says Max Dixon. Smooth, unbroken gestures convey positive emotions. Jerky gestures have an unsettling effect. You may have a place in your talk that calls for a rapid, jerky gesture. If so, use one. A steady stream of such gestures will make you look pontifical and contentious. If you can do a little yoga or stretch out without wrinkling your suit before you perform, you're more likely to be fluid and relaxed in your movement.

Think how some of your favorite athletes exhibit effort and control at the same time. Marcus Allen, one of the NFL's all time leaders in total yards, always looked balanced and in complete control of his body movement. Other running backs were bigger or faster, but none better at keeping their weight over their legs so as to make split second adjustments. Hakeem Olijuwon, at a mere 6' 10", is short by NBA standards for a center. Yet he consistently outplays taller opponents who lack his quickness and fluidity. Ozzie Smith is another athlete who made everything look easy, not just because of his extraordinary natural talent, but because he stayed relaxed even while leaping over a sliding base runner to turn a double play.

We can't all be as at ease in mid-performance as Mohammed Ali, Chris Evert, or Wayne Gretsky—other athletes who mastered staying within themselves. Yet we can be the most relaxed "us" possible if we set our mind to it and make the effort.

Chapter 13
PERSUASION

The Most Difficult Speech To Give

Persuasion is the most demanding kind of public speaking. For that reason, I have devoted a separate chapter to it even after commenting on it in other chapters.

Persuasion means changing people's beliefs or bringing about some action on their part. For a speaker to accomplish either of these objectives, the audience needs to be interested in the subject or issue. If the audience is not already interested, the speaker has the additional burden of generating interest. That's why some speakers, including me, believe that a hostile audience is preferable to an indifferent one. At least a hostile audience cares about the matter at hand—and probably knows something about it. That spares the speaker the often daunting task of generating interest.

In order for a speaker to change the way an audience thinks or to make individuals take an action, he or she must deliver both a message the audience understands and remembers. The audience must also believe that the speaker has its interests at heart. Of course, interests need not be limited to some tangible benefit, such as more money or better sex. It can mean moral interest, doing the right thing in accordance with one's own ethical standards. If someone demonstrates to you that a particular course of action is dictated by one of your professed, deeply held beliefs about right and wrong, he has done you a favor. He has helped you to become the kind of person you want to be, and he has shown you how to act in a way that is consistent with your values. That is in your moral interest.

Changing a Person's Beliefs or Actions

A speaker needs to know as much as possible about an audience's position in order to change the audience's beliefs or prompt an action. When you give a persuasive speech, first ask yourself exploratory questions. Are most or all of the audience likely to be for or against my stance? How firm are their beliefs? What led them to their beliefs?

Fear, prejudice, self-interest (greed, power, vanity, etc.), misinformation, indignation, or a laudable value (equality, tolerance, aesthetics, religious conviction, etc.)—any or all of these contribute to people's belief systems. Use what you know about the audience to devise an effective strategy for reaching them.

For example, if you know that a neighborhood association wants to prevent a merchant from getting a liquor license for his restaurant because the members think it will create public drunkenness, you address that issue. A talk about the morality or lack thereof of consuming alcohol would not be effective since that isn't the association's concern. They're not anti-alcohol; many of them may drink. They simply fear that restaurant patrons may abuse the privilege. An obvious strategy would be to show that in similar neighborhoods where a restaurant serves alcohol, no drunkenness problem exists. In fact, neighboring businesses have benefited from the additional people the restaurant attracts.

Let's take a weightier case, capital punishment. We needn't go through all, or even most, of the arguments for and against it. The important thing for a speaker trying to persuade an audience one way or the other is: Why do they adhere to the position they do? In any randomly selected audience, some people will believe in capital punishment and others will oppose it.

You will find different reasons for their positions among both the pros and the cons. Suppose you knew in advance that the pro-capital punishment people held their position on grounds of social pragmatism: tougher sentences will reduce crime. To argue against capital punishment on religious grounds (no one is beyond redemption), humanitarian grounds (any taking of human life is cruel), or democratic grounds (the penalty is not applied evenly across racial and socioeconomic lines) would not be very effective.

It would be more to the point—the audience's point—to show that no correlation between tougher sentencing and crime reduction exists, and that the cost of litigation makes it cheaper to incarcerate a person for life than to execute him.

You need data to make this kind of case or any other. For example, a Duke University study found that executions cost states nearly six times that of keeping a person in jail for life. You want to make your claim on the basis of information. Of course you could appeal to authority, the Bible or U.S. Constitution, but that won't carry weight with anyone who doesn't already acknowledge the authority. (How the relevant passages are to be interpreted is another whole can of worms, as both Bible and Constitutional scholars well know.) Data, or information, is vital to any persuasive speech.

Appeal to Reason

A second element of persuasion is reason. Every time we say to someone, "Use your common sense," we're appealing to reason. Some different ways to use reason in a persuasive speech are:

1. Reasoning from solution criteria.

State a problem. If the audience doesn't know about the problem, the solution won't mean anything to them. Once the audience knows the problem and how it affects them, state the criteria for an acceptable solution. Then show that your proposed solution meets the criteria.

This works well with hostile audiences because it allows you to establish some common ground (the criteria) before you announce your solution. Pointing out what you agree about before getting into what you disagree about diminishes the audience's hostility and demonstrates how reasonable you are.

2. Reasoning from analogy.

State the problem and tell how the same or a similar problem was overcome elsewhere with the solution you propose. This is the "It worked there; it'll work here" method. Be alert to the differences in the situations and how they might affect the likelihood of your solution succeeding. Lawyers reason from analogy when they cite previous cases and opinions. They know that if opposing counsel can show that the dissimilarities in the cases cited weaken the analogy, then their argument probably won't fly.

3. Reasoning from comparative advantage.

If everyone agrees that things as they are are insufferable, the speaker need only show that they will improve if the audience adopts his proposal. Such an approach has the advantage of not requiring rabid support, just agreement that the proposed change will have more value than doing nothing. The speaker can strengthen his case by showing that his solution is better than any other alternative, or the only one that will work.

It is always a good idea to address alternative solutions. It shows that you're aware of them, which enhances your credibility. It also gives you a chance to shoot them down, to show that they are based on misleading, incomplete or irrelevant information, faulty reasoning or mere speculation. That makes your solution shine in comparison.

What these three kinds of structure share is that you state the pain and sell the cure. You point out what's wrong, not working, holding us back, keeping us from realizing our personal or financial potential. Then you offer the best solution and why we can rely on it.

Tell a Story

The strongest persuasive structure is a story. You can build your argument around a story, or at least a theme. That does not exclude the kinds of reasoning we've just looked at. It can include one or more. Stories carry their own internal logic, a sequence of events, a plot. What better way to state a problem than with a brief story that contains both fact and action—truth that is simple and graphic. I witnessed an example of storytelling used as powerful persuader at the last political caucus meeting I attended. The group was divided on which of two senatorial candidates to support. Some favored the front-runner. Others leaned toward an underdog who better represented their views.

A woman who works with AIDS patients in hospices throughout the city spoke. "I went to Washington last year to seek support for our AIDS program. No one would talk to me, not a single one of our state's legislators. Without a base from which to operate, without a single friend in Congress who could get me a ten-minute audience with a colleague or two, I came home with nothing, not even a little hope.

"Every day I visit dying people, watch them die, and I can't tell them that help may be on the way, if not in time for them then maybe for those who will follow. That's why I'm asking you to vote for my guy. He is the only candidate who has a chance of winning against our well-financed opponent in the other party. Please, my friends, help to get us a senator who will consider the plight of people wasting away and at least talk to me when I go begging for funding for hospices and AIDS research."

It worked. All but one of the underdog's supporters voted for the front-runner. What credibility is to a speaker, electability is to a candidate. In its absence, little else matters. A persuasive speech is only as effective as the speaker is credible. A carefully crafted argument, replete with solid, relevant information and sound reasoning falls flat unless people believe the person who says it. That leads us to the third element of persuasion: passion.

The Emotional Element

Audiences want to know that we believe what we say, that we are sincere. If we fail to show them that we identify with our message, that we are persuaded by our own argument, and that we offer it to them not for our own but for their best interest, they won't give us the full measure of their trust. This is the personal element of persuasive speaking, the part that has to do with making people feel safe and appreciated, important and respected.

Remember: We let our emotions make most decisions, then look for reasons to justify the decisions. A speaker who tries to persuade people without appealing to their emotions had better have heaven on his side and heaven's signed, notarized position statement in hand.

We've talked elsewhere about some of the ways to achieve credibility by demonstrating sincerity. A few are worth repeating.

1. Give lots of eye contact.

Our eyes actually contain some brain cells. The pathways that run from the eyes to the brain are much larger than those between the ears and brain. The eyes are the only part of our body that has direct contact with the same body part of our listeners. Eyes are more than windows of the soul; they are gateways to the brain. We ignore their power at our peril.

2. Our posture reflects our self-esteem.

Stand tall. Let energy emanate from your body.
An exercise I do with clients is to have them send
their spirit into all part of the room. Breathing
deeply, they feel themselves expanding into the
spaces behind, in front and to the sides of them.
Invariably this empowers them in a way that talk
about voice projection and keeping one's head high
does not.

3. Our smile and gestures reveal us as open or
closed.

Have fun and you'll smile often and naturally. A
fake smile does more harm than none at all. We may
at least regard the dour as morally serious. The
phony we quickly relegate to the trash heap of
persuasive impotence.

4. Vary your voice.

Use it the way you'd drive a fine car on a
country road. Vary the speed, volume, pitch and
intensity. That makes you sound more natural and
adds interest to your delivery. The ear quickly tires
of the same rhythm, as the eye does of the same
facial expression, hand gesture or body movement.

5. Admit the downside of your argument.

A confession from your mouth is better than
exposure from another's. Lawyers know this better
than anyone.

I remember a trial in which an accomplice to a
murder turned state's evidence. The prosecutor put
him on the stand and asked about his long criminal
record. Every conviction and stint in prison came to
the jury's attention from questions on direct

examination, not cross examination. That robbed the defense of the chance to "expose" the witness as the unsavory fellow he was. By presenting information that was potentially injurious to his case, the prosecutor appeared more believable. In his closing argument, he made sure to distance himself from the witness. "We don't like him," he said, "and we don't expect you to. We had him testify because he was there and saw what happened, and he now has more to lose by lying than by telling the truth."

Roger Dawson, author of *Power Persuasion*, thinks it is unnecessary to present the downside of your argument if you have a friendly audience that will hear only from you and not an advocate of an opposing side. I disagree. To admit the weakness in your argument is both ethically responsible and tactically sound. Just because no one else is scheduled to speak in favor of an opposing position doesn't mean audience members won't be exposed to it. They read papers, watch television, talk to each other, and regularly use their own powers of reason. Why risk appearing ignorant of the weaknesses in your position or, worse, afraid to 'fess up to them. That does for your credibility what talking too long does for your popularity.

6. Use humor if it comes easily.

Humor prevents boredom and endears a speaker to an audience. We like people who make us laugh and we believe people we like. The best humor arises out of the material or situation at hand. Leave canned jokes, unless they relate to the topic, to professional comedians.

You may fail in your mission if humor becomes

the focus of a persuasive talk. The goal of your presentation is to persuade, not entertain. Hilarity can become an obstacle to thought. Who wants to grapple with facts and logic when they can sit back and laugh?

7. Never overstate.

Overstatement is a form of falsehood and a credibility killer. Speak only of genuine threats, not every one that could possibly arise from failing to adopt your position or take the action you urge. Predict only realistic rewards. If you promise more than can be reasonably expected, it undermines your sincerity.

8. Draw conclusions.

Either draw conclusions for your audience or make sure you have presented enough information so that they can draw the desired conclusion for themselves. Listeners are more strongly persuaded if they feel they reached a conclusion on their own. For that reason, sometimes it's better to let them do just that, especially if they are highly intelligent. Highly intelligent people have the reasoning skills to get themselves to the logical conclusion. Less intelligent audiences need both more guidance and emotional prodding.

Sometimes you have to point out the fallacious nature of an opponent's reasoning. A firm grasp of logic, including logical fallacies, is important to anyone who tries to persuade audiences that have heard or will hear the counter argument.

I remember a courtroom scene in which a prosecutor spoke of three facts and said, "Considered alone, none of these facts points to a conclusion. By itself, each is nothing. But when we consider them together, they form a strong case for the defendant's guilt." The jurors looked impressed; some even nodded. When it was the defense counsel's turn to speak, he retorted, "What a peculiar mathematical system the prosecutor would have you subscribe to. He admits that each of the three facts he has put before you amounts to nothing. Then he says that together they are evidence of my client's guilt. Since when does nothing plus nothing plus nothing make something?"

9. A call for action.

If you are calling for an action, be very clear about what action you want people to take. The more limited and specific your request, the more likely people are to perform it. If you tell smokers to give up their habit, you are less likely to get an immediate or long-term result than if you ask them to stop for only one day. Stopping for a day is less drastic. After a one-day hiatus, they may choose to refrain for another day. Likewise, if you ask people to vote for all candidates of a particular party, it will be less effective than asking them to vote for one or two who strongly embrace a laudable value.

Chapter 14
AUDIENCE RELATIONS

Connect With the Audience
Whatever the goal of our speech, we need to connect with our audience to reach that goal. People tend to listen better to speakers they like, speakers with whom they feel they have a connection—a relationship.

Some speakers assume that the relationship starts when they take the platform and utter their first sentence. I prefer to spend time with individual members of an audience before I take the platform. If you can make friends with some of the crowd ahead of time, you gain in three ways.

First, a few people will feel connected to you before you even open your mouth. That's money in the bank for a speaker. The better people like you, the more they'll forgive you. Sooner or later, no matter how good you are, you'll need the benefit of the doubt about something. It may be as trivial as your hair style or as consequential as your mind set, but you'll need it. We all do. The way to get it is to be liked.

Second, talking with people in advance gives you a chance to learn special interests or concerns they have. If you hadn't planned to address these matters in your talk, you can adapt your presentation to take them into account. Not only does this make your talk more relevant to your listeners, it shows you to be a caring person, someone who is sensitive to audience needs instead of stuck on your own agenda. You've only to mention that you were talking with so-and-so before the program and heard how concerned the group is about whatever. Before you even say something about that whatever, you've won the hearts of your audience.

Third, you've had a chance to identify sources of energy. As a speaker, you cherish listeners who give you energy—by facial expression (especially smiles), body language, eye contact. Some people will listen passively, others with abandon. Those who nod approval at your logic, laugh uninhibitedly at your humor, lean forward and beam when you look at them are sources of energy. They make your job easier—and much more fun. Every time you look at one of them, you'll get a lift.

When you spend time acquainting yourself in advance with people who'll be in your audience, you'll get a good idea which of them will serve you as empowerers when you address the group. I like the idea of looking at one of them before you say anything, then speak your first sentence—or even whole thought—to that person. That way you'll get the strongest, most energized start possible.

Here are some tips for introducing yourself to people.

1. Establish eye contact and smile before you extend your hand. That gives your subject a second to prepare him or herself for the introduction.

2. Extend your hand without breaking the eye contact and say your name. Continue to smile while

the other person says his or her name.

3. Have a firm but not overbearing grip. Make sure your thumb web contacts the other person's. Maintain the grip for a few seconds, if the other person permits you to. Hold the smile and eye contact. Both the smile and eye contact are crucial. They show that you're engaged, interested, focused and friendly—in short, likable, maybe even charismatic.

If you fear that your eye contact will come across as aggressive staring, just note the eye color of your new acquaintance. That gets your eyes on his or hers without the appearance of staring.

4. Hold yourself upright with your weight equally distributed on each foot. A little bend in your knees will both relax you and stop you short of military stiffness. The way you hold yourself goes a long way toward creating a positive impression.

As soon as the introduction is complete, ask why the person came to the presentation, seminar or meeting. If the answer doesn't point to a special and specific interest, go ahead and ask, "Is there something in particular you'd like to see addressed?" or, "What could I cover that would be of the most interest or help to you?"

Once I gave a talk to stockbrokers about using service as a selling technique. Originally, I had no plans to deal with telemarketing. When I talked to some of the brokers before the presentation, I learned that many of them solicit customers they've never met over the phone. Consequently, I made sure to include something about telephone manners. Then I followed it with an observation about the merits of face-to-face contact for developing relationships of trust.

Share The Stage
    Audience participation is another aspect of audience relations. More and more professional speakers, especially those with an educational mission, utilize their audiences as a resource. When you invite people to participate in the program, either by asking questions, sharing information, or demonstrating something, you make friends of them. We all like to feel included. We also like it if someone expresses appreciation for our concerns or contributions. So share the stage whenever you can. Your very willingness to let others into the spotlight will endear you to your audience.

    Here are some tips for using audience participants.

    1. Advise people in advance that you will call for volunteers. That gives them time to think about whether or not they want to volunteer. It also increases the likelihood that hands will go up as soon as you ask for them. (Calling for volunteers and getting none creates an embarrassment for you and your audience.) If you designate a "volunteer" you risk putting the person on the spot. That could offend him and everyone else. It's better to say something like, "In a few minutes, those of you who would like to can take part in a little demonstration of what we've been talking about."
    Since I do a lot of workshops on presentation skills, most of the volunteers give short speeches on a topic of their choice. I then prepare the audience

to give specific kinds of feedback, such as, "First, I'd like you to tell the speaker what you liked about the speech. Then let's comment on the eye contact, the opening, the speaker's posture and enthusiasm."

I have found this is much more effective than calling for general feedback. It gives the audience particular things to observe and address. That makes it easier for them and reinforces the ideas I want them to take away with them. If someone comments that the speaker seemed hesitant or emotionally detached, I'll ask the person who made the comment to identify the body part or mannerism that gave that impression. Did it come from hand gestures, vocal inflection, shoulder position, or some other body location? This helps the receiver of the feedback to correct the impression by using more decisive gestures or vocal variety, standing straighter or giving more eye contact.

2. Any volunteer, no matter how eager, is vulnerable. Protect his or her vulnerabilities. Thank people for their participation, not just outcomes. Some outcomes will be better than others. But all who volunteered deserve thanks for having done so.

You can also protect vulnerabilities by stating in advance that the purpose of the exercise is to have fun. That provides a face-saver (to you as well as the participant) in case the participant doesn't perform as well as you—and he or she—would have liked. Thank the participant and acknowledge him or her for having been willing to take a risk. Make the people feel that they contributed to the program. They did.

3. Let volunteers know exactly what you expect from them. Practice your directions and hone them until they are simple and succinct. Unclear directions create confusion, which quickly brings tension, even irritation. If you lack clarity in your instructions it can make you look incompetent. I've learned, through sometimes painful experience, to ask if everyone understands my directions. Even that's no guarantee they do, but it is far better than assuming they do. Assumption is the mother of misunderstanding.

4. Take volunteers and questions from all parts of the room. If someone in the back has a hand up, make every effort to include that person. People in the back are more likely to feel excluded if not called on more than those in the front.

5. If someone asks a question to which you don't know the answer or don't feel you can respond intelligently, ask if someone else would like to answer it. Admitting that you don't know everything creates credibility. It also allows you to let someone else shine. Of course, if your subject is rocks and you can't explain the difference between sandstone and granite, you could be in trouble. At least know the difference between "sentimental" and "disingenuous" rocks.

6. Start with easy exercises before asking people to do something that may be threatening. The one-minute nonverbal eye contact exercise described in the chapter titled "Games to Play" works better if people have already gotten comfortable with each other. Thrusting a difficult

exercise on an audience too early can freak out some people.

7. Give gifts to people who participate, especially if they are the first to try something or attempt a particularly difficult task. Giving gifts is fun, inexpensive and a great rapport builder. I always allot at least one percent of my fee for gifts. It's a terrific investment.

Including audience members as participants in your program creates a more intimate mood and greater immediacy. People will like you for letting them get involved, express themselves and have fun. By handing some control over to audience members, you show yourself to be a giving person, one who's willing to trust other people and let them share the stage. Do it and your sincerity soars!

Chapter 15
AUDIO/VISUAL ADVICE

TV Has Changed Us
Electronics have changed the way we view things. Think about the TV remote. It has drastically reduced the average American's attention span. That is why political sound bites have become ever shorter. We just won't stay tuned in to one thing as long as we used to. If it doesn't dazzle us instantly, we're out of there.

Another result of high tech—whether in movie special effects, state of the art fireworks, animation, or rock concert colored lights—is that audiences expect more. Fewer and fewer people are willing to sit in an auditorium and just listen to a well-prepared, intelligent, clearly delivered talk. Unless the speaker is already a hero to them, or they have a stake in absorbing the information the speaker came to impart, they want more than a little mental stimulation. They want to have fun. The savvy speaker makes sure they do.

Audio/Visuals Aid Presentations
Audio/visuals are one way of providing more fun for an audience. Used intelligently, they can enhance an already good presentation. One way they do this is to make points clearer through illustration. It's the old "picture worth a thousand words" theory. What we see and hear we are more likely to remember than that which we hear only. If

you are teaching something as complicated as ballistics or baseball to Balinese bushmen, you need diagrams. Ask yourself how you would explain baseball with words only to someone with no experience of the game. The rules alone present an incalculable verbal obstacle, much less the six different ways to exercise a double steal.

Audio/visuals can also be used to enhance a presentation and jazz it up. Music, cartoons, story boards, and colored overheads can add entertainment value and give more punch to your program. They are also useful to show products you may have for sale. This saves you from having to describe your back table inventory in a way that makes you look like a hawker.

Audio/visuals can also overwhelm you, either by making you look like a bit player in your own production or by occupying so much of your attention to operate them that you lose touch with your audience. Like any other machine, they can also fail you.

With these ideas in mind, here are some tips about audio/visuals:

1. Use them as tools, not crutches. Never let them upstage you. You are the alive one, the moving, thinking, breathing human being who can connect with other human being. The best audio/visual tools ever devised are your voice and your body.

2. Always be prepared to put on a show without them. Bulbs burn out, circuits break, extension cords don't quite reach, computers go on

strike. You forget some critical apparatus. The sponsor tells you that they have a projector; when you get to the site they tell you they can't find it— or it broke. He who lives by the tool sometimes dies by it. The less you use (and spare parts you have to carry), the less liability you have. When in doubt, leave it out.

3. Rent sophisticated equipment before you buy it. It's foolish to invest in something until you know it meets your needs and mechanical comfort level. Audio/visual technology is advancing so rapidly that by the time you return the rented equipment, something better may be available.

4. Make sure visuals are both visible and visual. Great graphics do nothing if people can't see them. Putting text without graphic embellishment on a slide or overhead is a waste of time. All visuals should make a visual statement.

5. Instead of writing on a flip chart and having to turn your back to the audience, invite an audience member to play stenographer for the group. Or, better yet, get two audience members, one right and one left handed, to stand on the sides of adjacent flip charts and write in turn points you or the audience provides.

6. Use technology the way you use words— with a purpose in mind. It becomes a distraction when used for its own sake rather than in service of your message. What you may gain in entertainment you risk losing in credibility. You could come across like one of those television painting teachers who

has an arsenal of clever techniques and nothing to present with them but minimally plausible, totally predictable trees and some "happy" clouds. A little sizzle helps sell your substance. Undue sizzle looks too slick. Your energy, not that of your machines, is what your audience wants most of all. Be your own primary resource and last resort. You are the unique human presence who can reach out and touch people.

Chapter 16
HANDOUTS

To Give or Not To Give Handouts

This is a difficult chapter for me to write because I don't like handouts. Most strike me as a waste of paper, and thereby a waste of trees. The most useful thing I carry away from other people's presentations are the notes I take. Taking notes forces me to participate in an active way. I record what's useful to me and let the rest slide by. Sure, something that might have been useful may elude me, but it probably isn't in the handout either.

A kind of handout popular with many speakers is one replete with blanks to fill in. These are sometimes confusing. Which word goes in which space? Which of the seven essentials of good speaking did I miss? Half the time I don't know. When I look around, I see other people looking at their neighbor's handout for a clue as to what information goes where. What an irony that in the so called "Information Age" people have lost the will to take their own notes and come to expect a handout that tells them what they are supposed to have learned from a program.

Points To Consider About Handouts

Some handouts are very useful. A list of good books on your topic will be welcomed by those few who want to know more about it. Your card makes it easy for folks to reach you. Blank paper gives those who didn't bring their own something to write notes on. An outline may make it easier for people to follow your talk.

Here are some general recommendations about handouts.

1. Pass them out either before or after your presentation, whichever is appropriate. If you want the audience to refer to the handout during your talk, obviously you distribute it in advance. When you give written material to people, the first thing they do is start to read it. That takes their attention away from you. If you give them a chance to look it over before you start, you spare yourself a nasty distraction.

2. If you distribute material after your presentation, do so by having it available and inviting people to pick it up if they're interested. Why give something to someone who has no interest in it and will throw it in a round file soon thereafter. Don't have your last act be to pass out of pieces of paper. Can you think of a weaker way to end?

3. Have your name, address and phone number on everything you give out. That way people who misplace your card still have something that tells them how to reach you if they wish to purchase your service or product—or just to invite you to dinner. Don't laugh; it happens!

4. Relate your handouts to your topic. An important reason for the handout is to reinforce

your message, often by making it more graphic through lively, even humorous, illustrations. It's silly to give a list of affirmations, no matter how soul-bending, to an audience that came to hear you talk about solar heating.

5. Never read your handout to the audience. You may call their attention to a particular page or section. It's an insult to their intelligence to read to them what they can read for themselves.

6. Beware of the overly flashy handout. It may prove an attention stealer. A handout, like slides and overheads, is a learning tool, not the heart of the matter. It's a gift from you to each audience member, something tangible they can take home. As such, it represents you and is a token of your esteem for your audience. But it is not you, and you have to stay the star.

Chapter 17
GAMES THAT ENLIVEN PRESENTATIONS

Audience involvement is critical to a presentation of an hour or more. Mark Twain said, "No sinner was ever saved after the first twenty minutes of a sermon." What I think he meant is that twenty minutes is the attention span of most people. Shifting gears every twenty minutes makes it easier for you audience to stay tuned. Robert Pike, a noted authority on the subject, recommends involving people every eight minutes. Pace changes generate energy. The best way to involve an audience is to give them something to do. Games and exercises are a sure-fire way to keep people interested. They can also help people to bond, generate information, reinforce learning, increase energy, improve retention, and promote discussion.

Some of my favorites are:

I. Partner Introduction

Have everyone find a partner, preferably someone they don't know already. Allow a minute each for them to interview each other, then introduce their partner to the whole group, if it's not more than ten or twelve people, or to other members of a smaller group. This exercise is useful as an "ice-breaker," something to loosen folks up, get them talking to each other. I never feel that there's any ice to break, and use the exercise as a foil for another introduction exercise.

II. No Darn Data Introduction

Introduce a partner after only a thirty second interview. No data—job, marital status, age, number of children, leisure activity—are allowed in the introduction. The idea is to present your personal impression of your partner in a convincing way, to share your feeling about the person. I like to use the exercise near or at the end of a program, after participants have already gotten to know each other. Questions that elicit information that helps to formulate the introduction are: What do you most love? Fear most? If you could be any animal, what would you choose? Any car? Any dessert?

There's no need to tell the audience what any of those choices are. It's more fun to infer what you like from the response and improvise on it. For example, if your partner, Glenda, says she'd like to be a dolphin, you might say: Glenda is a very social person with a love of play. She likes people and feels comfortable in different environments, especially those in which she can be active. She is very loyal to her family and also welcomes contact with strangers that reciprocate her friendliness.

What you say is less important than how you say it. The intro isn't supposed to be a complete psychological profile, just a passionate presentation of something you believe to be true about your partner. I find it works better if, after explaining it, I give a demonstration.

III. The Story of Something on Your Body

Tell a partner about something on or in your body—a piece of clothing, jewelry, scar, tattoo, hip replacement (I have one!). Take only a minute or two. Some of these stories may be worth sharing with the rest of the audience. One of the best I've heard was that of a woman named Ann, who told about her earrings. When she was nineteen, her fiancee jilted her for another woman. Twenty year later, after Ann had married and later divorced another man, someone knocked on her door. She opened it and there stood her former fiancee, a bouquet in one hand, a small box in the other. "Ann," he said, "I made a terrible mistake when I broke our engagement. Please take me back and be my wife."

"Come in and let's talk," said Ann. Two weeks later they got married. Ann wears the earrings, which were in the little box, wherever she goes.

IV. Anecdote or Challenge Exchange

Tell a partner something good that happened to you in the last week, or tell about a challenge you are facing, why it's a challenge, and your strategy for dealing with it. This exercise takes very little time. I find the game useful to show people how they can start or keep a conversation going after the customary exchange of names.

V. Three Things in Common

This game encourages people to open up with each other. I've found it especially effective with singles groups. It takes a while to play, even with a small audience, but the energy it generates and the laughs it produces are well worth it.

Find a partner and take five minutes to discover the three most interesting things you have in common. Sun signs, job similarities (unless the jobs are very unusual), and recreational activities are not interesting. Go for things very few people would have in common, like an exotic, out-of-the-way place you've both been or the fact that as kids you both raised snakes. When the partners have gotten their three things (two things for groups of three people), I have them announce their commonalties and write them on a flip chart. Then the whole group votes on the winners, to whom I give prizes. In one group the winners were two women who found they'd both been pregnant in Beaumont, Texas. In another, it was a man and woman who had both wet their pants in fourth grade classes.

An important benefit of the game is that it is an object lesson in active listening. With prizes at stake, people really pay attention to what their partner is saying, lean forward and ask questions. That, I tell them, is the best way to listen to anyone—fully focused on what he or she is saying.

VI. Observation Exercise

Again with a partner, take ten seconds to look at each other. Then turn your backs to each other and make a slight change in your appearance—put a ring on a different finger, loosen your tie, ruffle your hair, remove a necklace. See if your partner notices the change. This quickie exercise has little educational value but can add a little fun to a stretch break.

VII. Six Person Introduction

This is the best way I know to energize an audience in which most people don't already know each other. If the audience has been sitting for a while, listening to announcements or another speaker, I find an excuse to use it.

Give people ninety seconds to stand up and introduce themselves to six others they haven't already met. The time limit means they have to keep moving, looking for new people to introduce themselves to. In one group, a man climbed on his chair to get a better view of who was around him. People started coming to him. It added to the semi-chaotic, manic energy in the room. When you call time at the end of ninety seconds, you'll see that everyone in the room is smiling.

If you want to glean some educational value from the exercise, ask the audience which of them noticed the eye color of the people they introduced themselves to. Who remembered the most names? Who had a tactile memory of the grips? How many were aware of the firmness of their own grip?

This can be an introduction of things to do when you meet people: look them in the eye, focus on their names, maintain a firm but not hurtful grip for a few seconds, stand up straight, SMILE.

VIII. Body Language Game

With a partner find a topic on which you agree and one about which you disagree. Any topic will do—the best place to live, the wisdom of welfare reform, the ideal pet. First discuss the topic on which you agree while one partner does things to undermine the rapport, such as turning his back, interrupting, not giving eye contact, using words like "but," "must" and "you'll have to." Next discuss the topic about which you disagree. One partner models the body language of the other, gives eye contact, paraphrases what his partner said then says "and" to preface his own contribution to the discussion.

Then compare the rapport levels in the two conversations. Everyone with whom I've ever played the game reports that an agreeable disagreement produces far better vibrations than a disagreeable agreement. The purpose of the game is to sensitize us to the importance of body language and word choices for establishing and maintaining rapport with anyone with whom we communicate.

IX. Eye Contact Exercise

Sit facing a partner with your knees not more than four inches apart. Put your hands on your knees. Give each other sixty seconds of eye contact without any words, gestures or specific facial expressions, like smiles. The exercise tests one's comfort level with eye contact. Blinking is fine; this is not a contest to see who blinks first. It's an opportunity simply to hang out with a partner.

I often make it easier for people by telling them first to note the other person's eye color, then to send them a positive thought. This takes the attention away from one's own nervousness or discomfort and puts it on the partner. As with all exercises, I then debrief the audience, ask if someone will share with the group how it felt, what the experience was like, if any insight emerged. A frequent and welcome response is: after doing that I think I'll have a much easier time giving people eye contact when I talk to them.

X. Story-Telling Game

Divide people into groups of four or five. In turn let each tell a personal anecdote of about two minutes. It's important that it be personal, not a joke or story about someone else. Have other members of the small group keep their hands up until the speaker has given each at least five seconds of continuous, sustained eye contact. Two seconds now, three seconds later doesn't get the hand down.

The game, which is technically an exercise, encourages both eye contact and sharing of oneself. Each group needs a timekeeper to signal people when two minutes has elapsed and a monitor to see that one story follows another directly without discussion of the stories. It's hard enough to get groups to finish within five minutes of each other without such discussion. With discussion, things get way out of sync.

If time permits, I like the participants to tell each other what topic the story might make a good introduction to. My very favorite way to begin a presentation is with a personal story. Have the group choose its favorite story to turn the exercise into a game. Those stories get repeated to the whole audience and then popular vote determines a winner.

XI. Problem-Solving Exercise

Again in a small group, each person states a problem he or she has around an issue relevant to the program or seminar's focus. For example, in a communication seminar, someone might say, "I don't know how to handle people who interrupt me all the time." In turn, every other member of the group suggests a technique for dealing with interrupters.

XII. Teach Your Partner (or Group)

The best way to learn something is to teach it. We easily forget what we hear and read; we remember what we do. Give partners or members of small groups (four people max) an opportunity to instruct each other in specific points you've made. In a seminar on selling, for example, you've stressed the importance of initiative, imagination, and information. Let each person in a group of three take one of these ideas, define it and give at least two examples of how it can be implemented. It's fine that they may simply repeat what you've given them. In doing so they are internalizing your message. Some will expand on what you presented, think of other examples, maybe even call upon the other group members to come up with fresh applications of your principles. That's just what you want—audience involvement.

XIII. Follow-up Pledge

This isn't a separate exercise but rather something that can be added to any exercise that calls for participants to learn a new technique or implement a plan. The last exercise (#XII) would be

ideal for a follow-up pledge. Partners agree to call
each other in one week and inquire about the
results garnered by putting the technique or plan
into action. Knowing that someone will ask you
what you've done with what you learned is
powerful incentive to use the new ideas NOW.

XIV. Blind Date

One partner wears a blindfold and lets the
other guide him or her around and even out of the
room. The guide's job is to make the blind date feel
safe, provide discoveries (new or unusual tactile and
auditory experiences), and take care of the person.
Obviously, the guide has to be fully present and
attuned to the blindfolded partner. That's part of the
beauty of the exercise. The blindfolded partner's job
is to trust the guide and do whatever he or she asks.
This exercise has immediate relevance to programs
in team building, leadership, self-awareness,
sensitivity and the like. It helps strangers who will
work together on a project in or out of the
workshop to bond. I finish the exercise by having
the participants thank each other. Be sure to bring
enough blindfolds!

XV. Trust Fall

In a group of six to eight, form a circle with
one person standing in the center. Those standing
in the circle stand close together and hold hands.
The person in the middle shuts his eyes, either
crosses his arms or locks his hands in front of him,
and lets himself fall backward or to either side. The
people in the circle catch him. Everyone takes a

turn in the center. The exercise works well for the same kind of programs Blind Date does. I don't recommend it for captive audiences or people who are dressed up and may resent getting their clothes wrinkled. If every applicant for a management position had to pass this trust test, we'd have a happier work force. My feeling is that if a person doesn't trust other people to catch his fall of a few feet, he can't be trusted to lead a company, college, or military unit.

XVI. Two-Minute Back Rub

If your audience is seated in rows, ask them to stand and face the same direction, toward one side of the room or the other. When you say "Begin," each person gives the person in front of him a two minute back and shoulder massage. After two minutes, people reverse direction and rub someone else. The exercise works fine with partners, though a line rub is a bit less threatening to the touch wary. This is far more fun than a stretch break. I recommend using it only after you've had some less kinesthetic exercise that's served to acquaint people with their neighbors. Be sure to announce that no one is required to participate, so the touch phobics in your midst won't feel pressured to do something outside their comfort zone.

XVII. Three Important Points

An excellent activity for early arrivals while you wait for last minute arrivals is to have small groups decide three or four things they'd like to get from the program. It not only gives folks an activity, it gets them thinking about the program content. It also works well at the end of an extended program, seminar or class. In that case, you ask the groups to list the three most important things they learned and their reasons for choosing these over others. This helps to reinforce ideas. As with any exercise, debrief when you finish. Ask for the results, perhaps even write them on a flip chart.

XVIII. Self-Disclosure

One of the best get-acquainted games going is to have participants write the last word to seven statements:

When I was little I wanted to be _____.
Now I am _____.
Something I'd like to do better is _____.
My major source of grief is _____.
Something I do well is _____.
My major source of joy is _____.
Right now I feel _____.

Divide into small groups and have each person share his or her response to the first statement. Go around the group again for each succeeding statement. This method of going around the group for every statement is far superior to letting people go through all their statements at once. It keeps interest up, creates a little suspense as the statements become more revelatory, provides more opportunity to reinforce names, and goes a long way in getting people to bond. Because the exercise takes more time than most, it's most practical as an opener for longer programs or classes.

XIX. Different Values Demonstration

Individual people have different moral frames of reference. While we all agree that values like integrity, loyalty and honesty are good ones, we often find such values in conflict in a specific situation. Then we are forced to make difficult decisions about what is "right." Understanding how others analyze an ethically ambiguous situation is important to our appreciation of them as human beings.

Any program on leadership, communication, team building, or other interpersonal content can benefit from an exercise that gives participants a chance to share firmly held beliefs and how they apply them to a specific ethical problem.

Describe a dilemma. Here's an example I used to use in college philosophy classes. Dick and Jane have been married for sixteen years and have two children. He provides well for his family but has become increasingly involved in his work, so much in fact that he has long ignored his wife's emotional and physical needs. She has called this to his attention repeatedly but to no avail. Of these three alternatives for Jane—divorce, affair, grin and bear it—which is the least bad and why?

Divide into groups of four for discussion. Take twenty to thirty minutes. One group member is the secretary and takes notes. Another is the reporter who will share the group's "conclusion" with the larger group. Someone else is the captain and encourages all members to participate. The fourth person is the analyst. He or she asks questions of the others to clarify their reasoning. The reasons are more important than the conclusion. Part of the group report can be about what additional

information might have led to a different
conclusion.

No matter how many classes I've given this
problem to, one thing never changes. People
disagree. Even people who chose the same
"solution" did so for different reasons. Many said
that the exercise gave them a better understanding
of themselves and others.

XX. Who Goes First

This is not a game as such, just a way for a
group to have fun figuring out who will be first to
do whatever the assigned activity is. Just announce
that the first person will be any of the following:

Who was born closest (or farthest) from where
you now are?
Whose birthday is closest to today?
Who has the biggest feet?
Who has the longest hair?
Who is the oldest (or youngest)?
Who is the anything else you can think of?

Chapter 18
IMPROMPTU

Impromptu Speeches Can Be as Fun as Games

In the seminars I teach, two activities provide more fun than any others: the original commercial for an imaginary product and the impromptu speech.

People have fun with the commercial because they get to think of a product or service that would ease their life. They then build a short sales presentation around it, usually making it funny. I remember the lively commercial a single woman gave for what she called a creep detector. The imaginary gadget was no bigger than a computer mouse. When run down the side of a prospective date, it revealed such character traits as habitual lying, fear of commitment, dislike of his mother, and impatience with children.

Another memorable product was the clapper crapper, a toilet whose seat went up and down with hand commands to accommodate gender differences. One clap up, two claps down. No more marital arguments over who failed to leave the toilet seat properly positioned for whom when a couple invests in a clapper crapper.

Imaginative Impromptu Speeches

As much fun as the original commercial is the impromptu talk. I like to get suggestions from the group for topics that will let people spontaneously exercise their imaginations. Such topics include things like: bottled smiles, psychiatric service for pets, Essence of Man cologne, lunar cleaning supplies, travel ad for a town called Nowhere.

Since no one knows in advance what he will speak on, there's no time to get nervous. Speakers get their topic, have a few seconds to free associate while they walk to the front of the room, and let loose. What they find is that a single thought, presented naturally and with energy, is sufficient to carry the day. It drives home the point that anyone can be a good speaker if he is natural and lively.

For those who like an impromptu formula, here's a good one. Have a brief opening, state an idea, support the idea, close. Suppose your topic was designer pets from cross-species breeding. You could open with the time honored tradition of a question. "Have you ever wished you could combine the cuddly quality of a Koala bear, the sweetness of a golden retriever and the ferocity of, when needed, a Bengal tiger? Now you can."

Having set the stage with the opening, you proceed to your main point. "The Gene Jocks have developed a new genetic process called Insidious Insemination. It makes possible the pet combination of your fondest fantasy."

Support for the main point need be no more than examples of possible combinations. "Suppose you'd like a pet that catches mice and talks. We'll mix a python with a parrot, and your pythrot (or parthon, if you prefer) will fill that bill, if you'll pardon the pun. Or maybe you're yearning for a swimming companion that can lick your face. How about a porpoise crossed with a puppy. And if you want it to lay eggs, we'll chip in a chicken."

Now you're ready to close. "Whatever your designer pet desire, we can accommodate it. Just call The Gene Jocks at 1-800-STRANGE, and you can answer your friends incredulous questions every time you walk your whatever."

Serious Impromptu Speeches

The same formula works for a serious subject. Say your assignment is Flag Burning: Should It Be Legal? You could open with: "We love our flag and our Constitution. The debate about flag burning is about which we value more." Or: "Freedom of speech or protection for a national symbol—that's what the flag burning debate comes down to."

Next you state your thesis, or point. "I believe the Supreme Court was correct in striking down laws that prohibit flag desecration." Then give your support. "The Constitution, which is the cornerstone of our democracy, makes very clear that freedom of political speech is essential to that democracy. Besides this compelling political argument, there's an equally compelling practical argument. If we have laws against flag desecration, who is to say what constitutes such desecration? Does a flag motif on clothing? On a rug? On wallpaper? On toilet paper? How far can we reasonably go to 'protect' a symbol?"

Now close. "Rather than concern ourselves and our legislators with such hair splitting, let us turn our attention to more pressing matters. Even those of us who find flag burning abhorrent will admit that instances of it are rare and serve only to discredit the burners, not the burned."

IPAC Formula

Granted, it's easier to think of lines sitting at a computer than standing in front of a live audience. Yet if you keep the formula—Introduction, Point, Argument, Conclusion (IPAC)—in mind, you can give shape and coherence to any impromptu talk. Even if you lose the formula, ramble a bit till you run out of ideas and forget to close, you'll find that your words take flight if you deliver them with conviction. So never fear to wing it; you have all the resources you need to make a powerful, passionate impromptu, and have fun doing it.

Chapter 20
QUOTES OF NOTE

Wise Words To Use as Openers, Closers and In-Betweeners

Lovers are like empires: when the idea they are founded on crumbles, they, too, fade away.
Milan Kundera

We cannot transcend our shortcomings if no one lets us know what they are.
Matthew Arnold

Everything imagined is reality. The mind cannot conceive unreal things.
David Smith

The promise, the hint of new vista, the unresolved, the misty dream, the artist should love even more than the resolved, for here is the fluid force, the promise and the search.
David Smith

Force is the midwife of every old society pregnant with a new one.
Karl Marx

It would help very little if one persuaded millions of men to accept the truth, if precisely by the method of their acceptance they were transferred into error.
Soren Kierkegaard

A very popular error: having the courage of one's convictions. Rather it is a matter of having courage for an attack on one's convictions!
Friedrich Nietzsche

There is no fate that cannot be surmounted by scorn.
Albert Camus

Nobody should have to clean up anybody else's mess in this world. It's terribly bad for both parties, but probably worse for the one receiving the service.
Tennessee Williams

The public somebody you are when you 'have a name' is a fiction created with mirrors and the only somebody worth being is the solitary and unseen you that existed from your first breath and which is the sum of your actions and is so constantly in a state of becoming under your own volition.
Tennessee Williams

Real thinking is like real charity... it begins at home.
David Swenson

It is one thing for a sickness to be overcome, quite another thing for it to be merely lulled to sleep.
St. Augustine

Is it always an advantage to replace an indistinct picture by a sharp one? Isn't the indistinct one often exactly what we need?
Ludwig Wittgenstein

Orthodoxy is intellectual pharisaism.
Paul Tillich

Guilt and innocence are simply another categorical system with which we attempt with very poor success to deal with the continuing mystery of life.
Donald Winks

If men are to interest themselves for anything, they must... have part of their existence involved in it; find their individuality gratified by its attainment.
W. F. Hegel

Errors in religion are dangerous; those in philosophy only ridiculous.
David Hume

Truth, like certain precious metals, is presented best in alloys.
Philip Wheelwright

No man, for any considerable period, can wear one face to himself, and another to the multitude, without finally getting bewildered as to which may be the true.
Nathaniel Hawthorne

Your sexual virility is only the sign of a higher power you haven't begun to use.
Henry Miller

All men should strive to learn before they die what they are running from, and to, and why.
James Thurber

The accomplished cannot be annulled, but only confused.
Franz Kafka

Life is a hospital in which every patient is possessed by the desire to change his bed.
Baudelaire

Even bees, the little almsmen of spring-bowers,
Know there is richest juice in poison-flowers.
John Keats

We live amid surfaces, and the true art of life is to skate well on them.
Ralph Waldo Emerson

Faithfulness is to the emotional life what consistency is to the life of the intellect—simply a confession of failure.
Oscar Wilde

The man who is forever disturbed about the condition of humanity either has no problems of his own or has refused to face them.
Henry Miller

A man can't always be defending the truth; there must be a time to feed on it.
C. S. Lewis

The world tends to trap and immobilize you in the role you play; and it is not always easy—in fact, it is always extremely hard—to maintain a kind of watchful, mocking distance between oneself as one appears to be and oneself as one actually is.
James Baldwin

Some men see things as they are and say 'Why?' I dream things that never were and say 'Why not?'
George Bernard Shaw

Every man would like to be God if it were possible; some few find it difficult to admit the impossibility.
Bertrand Russell

You can be trapped by your own way. You should not try too hard.
Shunryu Suzuki

The chains of humanity are forged from administrative papers.
Franz Kafka

An action which wants to serve man ought to be careful not to forget him on the way.
Simone de Beauvoir

So long as the mind is seeking gratification, there is not much difference between God and drink.
J. Krishnamurti

The way to become human is to learn to recognize the lineaments of God in all of the wonderful modulations of the face of man.
Joseph Campbell

Every man's foremost task is the actualization of his unique, unprecedented and never recurring potentialities, and not the repetition of something that another, and be it even the greatest, has already achieved.
Martin Buber

The most effective way to live is as a warrior. Worry and think before you make any decision, but once you make it, be on your way free from worries or thoughts; there will be a million other decisions still awaiting you.

Carlos Castaneda

Without tradition, art is a flock of sheep without a shepherd. Without innovation, it is a corpse.

Winston Churchill

The creative act... is an act of getting out on a limb and of being extremely vulnerable, and this involves a kind of courage which resort to good taste might easily modify. The creative impulse involves a large ingredient of vulgarity to be a vital statement.

Robert Fawcett

You will never find yourself until you quit preconceiving what you will be when you have found yourself.

Robert Henri

In the high country of the mind one has to become adjusted to the thinner air of uncertainty.

Robert Pirsig

Until you know a good, Jewish middle-class, upwardly mobile, anxiety-ridden neurotic, you haven't met a real achiever!

Ram Dass

The only reality which a man can ever surely know is that self he cannot help being, though he will only know that self through its interactions with the world around it. If he pretties it up, if he changes its meaning, if he gives it the voice of any borrowed authority, if in short he rejects this reality, his mind will be less than alive.

W. D. Snodgrass

Human love flows easiest at a blurred object. Familiarity destroys illusions. Intimacy starts where romanticism ends.

Robert Capon

We all invent ourselves, but some of us are more persuaded than others by the fiction that we are interesting.

Janet Malcolm

The greatest fault...is to be conscious of none.

Thomas Carlyle

The 'silly' question is the first intimation of some totally new development.

Alfred North Whitehead

For one human being to love another: that is pehaps the most difficult task of all..., the work for which all other work is but preparation. It is a high inducement to the individual to ripen...a great exciting claim upon us, something that chooses us out and calls us to vast things.

Rainer Maria Rilke

Even if your on the right track, you'll get run over if you just sit there.

Will Rogers

Chapter 19
ON BECOMING WHO WE TRULY ARE:
AUTHENTICITY AS PRESENCE
AND RESPONSIBILITY

Our foremost responsibility as speakers is to share our human identity with our audience. That means we must have an identity, not borrowed bits and pieces of other identities we admire. The greatest gift we can give is that of ourselves, our point of view, and our labor. This is what I mean by authenticity.

We usually take authentic to mean congruence of thought and deed, or acting in accord with one's professed values. It's a valid definition, but the mere absence of hypocrisy just doesn't go far enough. To me, authenticity includes some other ideas, one of which is to be fully present. That means treating other people as ends, not means. One way we do that as speakers is to customize. Take time to develop fresh material for the particular needs and desires of each audience. It is a way of honoring the uniqueness of that group and being fully present.

For example, plan to have at least one new story for every audience. Dizzy Dean, the superb St. Louis Cardinal pitcher, used to give different, often conflicting stories to every reporter who interviewed him. Since television wasn't around yet, it took a while before someone confronted him with his inconsistencies. "They ain't exactly lies," said Dizzy. "I just try to give everybody somethin' original." To emulate Dizzy we needn't dissemble, just find a new pearl for every group.

Another way to be fully present is to serve your audience with all your heart, soul, and mind. Show up with all you've got and ready to be nowhere else. We're more than our power suit, super smile, terrific technique and colossal content. We're also our souls—all those longings, terrors, aspirations, appreciations, passions, and awakenings that contribute to our quintessential self. We're also products of our pasts, the choices we made and the circumstances, enriching as well as untoward, those choices created.

Let's bring to our work the dragons we battle as well as the resources that, now and again, permit us to prevail. This doesn't mean confessing things that will embarrass the audience for the sake of a personal catharsis. It means allowing ourselves to be who we are, including fallible, vulnerable and transient. The "I" who speaks is not a fixed thing but a work in progress that unfolds even as we speak.

To be fully present usually connotes paying absolute attention to the people we're with. I believe that until we bring all of ourselves to the task of attention, we don't meet the highest standard of presence. Let's call it being fully, fully present.

Another way to be authentic is to take responsibility for who and what we are—and accept ourselves as we are.

One way we demonstrate our self-acceptance is to rely heavily on our own experience. Research is a wonderful thing but no substitute for telling our own stories, especially those of which we are not the heroes.

Another way is to assume custody of our own introductions. An unprepped second party may under or overstate the case for listening to us, confuse fact until it's fiction, or accurately articulate the irrelevant. Part of our job is to see that the audience gets introduced to the us we really are.

The most important way we show self-acceptance is to forgive ourselves for having the identity we have, not some other, real or imagined, we may covet. I'd love to have Arnold Schwarzenegger's physical stature, James Earl Jones' gorgeous voice, the impish, twinkle-eyed smile of Michael Jordan or the sock-your-knocks-off one Sophia Loren beams at us. But I don't. All of us "only got what we got." And that's good enough if we just go with it—with all we've got. And one thing we all have is an unlimited capacity for authenticity—the heart and soul of effective communication.

THE TALK DOC'S TWELVE TIPS
FOR
POWERFUL, PASSIONATE PRESENTATIONS

1. Step lively to the platform. Look eager and energetic.

2. Get set physically before you start. Take a little time to look at specific members of the audience. Breathe deeply, then begin.

3. Begin with your first sentence, not "well," "uh" or "you know," and never with an apology. If you feel compelled to state why you aren't at your best—death, disease or other disaster—save it for the end and thank the audience for their indulgence. Never beg it in advance.

4. Speak every word to someone. If you need to consult your notes, do so silently. Then reestablish eye contact with a person and resume.

5. Let nothing stand between you and the audience unless absolutely necessary. Every physical barrier is a psychological barrier.

6. Write your material from the heart, speak it from the diaphragm. That lends sincerity to your word, and resonance to your voice.

7. Respect the autonomy of your listeners' minds and consciences. Provide all important data, even if it runs counter to your argument. Distorting or withholding relevant data kills your credibility.

8. Use stories to illustrate points. Everyone loves a good story.

9. Stand up straight. No fidgeting, swaying or leaning on anything. If nervous, simply act as though you are not.

10. Express enthusiasm for your topic with every instrument you have—your voice, body and face. Your listeners want evidence of your involvement with your subject and joy in sharing it.

11. Reciprocate applause by staying put and smiling rather than running for your seat right after your last word.

12. Prepare, prepare, prepare. Make your presentation a gift of your labor to others. Remember: every audience is sacred.